*Take Up Your
Mat and Walk*

# Take Up Your Mat and Walk

## Applying the Metaphor of Walking to the Spiritual Life

Mark Mah

WIPF & STOCK · Eugene, Oregon

TAKE UP YOUR MAT AND WALK
Applying the Metaphor of Walking to the Spiritual Life

Copyright © 2016 Mark Mah. All rights reserved. Except for brief quotations in critical publications or reviews, no part of this book may be reproduced in any manner without prior written permission from the publisher. Write: Permissions, Wipf and Stock Publishers, 199 W. 8th Ave., Suite 3, Eugene, OR 97401.

Wipf & Stock
An Imprint of Wipf and Stock Publishers
199 W. 8th Ave., Suite 3
Eugene, OR 97401

www.wipfandstock.com

PAPERBACK ISBN: 978-1-5326-0468-3
HARDCOVER ISBN: 978-1-5326-0470-6
EBOOK ISBN: 978-1-5326-0469-0

Manufactured in the U.S.A.                  SEPTEMBER 19, 2016

All truly great thoughts are conceived by walking.
—Friedrich Nietzsche


*Solvitur ambulando* (It is solved by walking)
—Medieval saying, attributed to St. Jerome

# Contents

*Introduction* | ix

Chapter 1. The Metaphor of Walking | 1

Chapter 2. The Call to Journey | 17

Chapter 3. An Embodied Spirituality | 31

Chapter 4. The Present Moment | 45

Chapter 5. The Gift of Wonder | 59

Chapter 6. The Hospitable Space | 74

Chapter 7. Solitude and Silence | 89

Chapter 8. The Simple Life | 103

*Bibliography* | 117

# Introduction

> Now there is in Jerusalem near the Sheep Gate a pool, which in Aramaic is called Bethesda and which is surrounded by five covered colonnades. Here a great number of disabled people used to lie—the blind, the lame, the paralyzed. One who was there had been an invalid for thirty-eight years. When Jesus saw him lying there and learned that he had been in this condition for a long time, he asked him, "Do you want to get well?" "Sir," the invalid replied, "I have no one to help me into the pool when the water is stirred. While I am trying to get in, someone else goes down ahead of me." Then Jesus said to him, "Get up! Pick up your mat and walk" (John 5:2–8).

THE PEOPLE AT THE pool have a reason to be there. They are looking for a cure. They have given up hope on the doctors of the day. They are all looking out for a miracle. Desperation drives them to this place. The chances are slim. They have problems of mobility. The blind cannot move quickly when the pool is stirred. The lame have difficulty walking. The invalid need others to help them move. Still they are there waiting for a miracle to take place. They all share one thing in common: all of them desire to get cured so that they can live a normal life.

When Jesus comes along no one is looking to him for a cure. This reception is quite unusual for Jesus because he is a well-known healer of diseases. Prior to this he has healed the dying son of an official. One person catches the eye of the teacher. His attention is on an invalid who has been there for a long time. Thirty-eight years to

## Introduction

be exact. Of all the people at the pool, this nameless invalid has the least chance to get cured. Jesus takes pity on this person and asks, "Do you want to get well?" A strange question indeed. Everybody at the pool want to get well. That is the reason they congregate in that place. There will always be a big crowd at anytime of the day. Permanent shelters are built in view of the popularity of the place. The answer given by the invalid to Jesus is equally strange. Instead of a Yes, the invalid comes up with an excuse on why he is not getting healed. He blames others for not helping him when the pool is stirred.

Many of us are like the disabled people at the pool. We are spiritually impotent and immobile. We are not happy with our spiritual condition and find excuses on why we are in such a state of spiritual lethargy. The excuses and blame are many. We are too busy to find time for spiritual matters. Family and work obligations take us away from God. We lack the thirst for spiritual matters. Spiritual matters are only for the elite. We have been disappointed by church members who do not walk the talk. We look for answers to our problems but our leaders are not able to help. The arrogance and hypocrisy of some brothers and sisters are too much to tolerate. When we really need help no one is there to give a lending hand.

The way to spiritual health is not to make excuses or put blame on others. We need to look into our hearts and ask ourselves whether we really want to get well. Do we *really want* to take this road of spiritual recovery at all cost? The desire is still there but it has been obscured and dimmed by layers of worldly concerns and spiritual neglect. If we are willing, Jesus will work through these layers to awaken the desire buried deep inside us. We are ready to take on a journey with God when we are awakened from the spiritual slumber

Jesus calls on the invalid to take up his mat and walk. He can easily walk away leaving his mat behind. He may not need the mat anymore. Someone else can take over his spot. A strategic spot is important to those at the pool in order to gain quick access to it when it is stirred. Does Jesus mean that by taking the mat he no longer comes back to the place anymore? Anyway, he is instructed to take up the mat before he walks away. A mat is a mobile bed. With a mat, or sleeping bag in our days, we are prepared to sleep at any place we can find. A sleeping bag is useful and necessary for those who are on the road. The road to spiritual health is to get ready our sleeping bags and walk with God to wherever he wants to take us. Are we willing to be walkers with God? Jesus finds the healed invalid at the temple and cautions him to stop sinning or something worse may happen to him (John 5:14). Now that his physical ailment is taken away he should also consider seriously the health of his own soul. Neglecting the health of his soul has eternal consequences.

The generational line running from Adam to Noah is recorded in the fifth chapter of Genesis. Names are mentioned with the same refrain: So and so lived for a number of years and bore a son. After he became a father he lived for a further number of years and had other sons and daughters. After living all together for the full number of years he died. The refrain of names goes on monotonously until we hit a bump. When we come to Enoch, the word "lived" changes to "walked". The phrase, "then he died" is replaced by another phrase, "he was no more because God took him away." Apparently, Enoch was different from the others on the list. While others just lived out their lives, Enoch lived by walking with God. He held a special place in God's heart for he was taken and did not die.

Do we want to just live out the full span of our lives? We do not care whether our lives will make a difference or not. Or, do we want to truly live by walking with God. The choice is ours to make.

*Chapter 1*

# THE METAPHOR OF WALKING

> I never do anything but when walking, the countryside is my study.
>
> —JEAN-JACQUES ROUSSEAU[1]

## Walk with Jesus

CHRISTIANS ARE CALLED TO walk by faith and not by sight. They are exhorted to walk in the light as Jesus is in the light. They are expected to walk in love and to walk humbly before God. Walking is a metaphor used in the Bible to depict the life or conduct of a believer. Christians ought to be walkers though many are not. They prefer a sedentary life and wonder why their spiritual life is at a standstill. Disciples are called to walk with Jesus. "Come, follow me," Jesus called out to them (Mark 1:17). By following him, Jesus showed them the way to the Father and his kingdom. Once Thomas asked Jesus, "Lord, we don't know where you are going, so how can we know the way?" Jesus replied that he was the way, the truth, and the life (John 14:5–6). No wonder the early Christians were called by others as those "who belonged to the Way"(Acts 9:2; 19:9). To belong to the "Way" we need to follow Jesus.

---

1. Cited by Gros, *A Philosophy of Walking*, 65.

## Take Up Your Mat and Walk

Jesus calls us to follow and walk with him on the path of life. Walking suggests a state of continued progress in a certain direction chosen by the walker. The disciples' walk with the master yielded spiritual results as they identified themselves with the work and mission of Jesus. Walking with God leads to growth in our spiritual life. It is mentioned in the Bible that Enoch and Noah walked with God for they were righteous in his sight. God commanded Abraham to walk before him and be blameless (Gen 17:1). In the Bible, the term "walking" is used metaphorically to describe a person's conduct and lifestyle. To walk with God is to abide by God's laws and to stay close to God's path (Isa 2:3). Conversely, we can choose not to walk with God. We prefer to walk in the counsel or the path of the wicked (Ps 1:1). Walking with Jesus will not lead us astray. Augustine had this advice for Christians in a sermon that he preached in the fifth century:

> Be in attendance at the manger; do not be ashamed of being the Lord's donkey. You will be carrying Christ; you will not go astray walking along the way because the Way is sitting on you.[2]

Our primary duty, as followers of Jesus, is to walk with him. Jesus was on the move all the time. Jesus, unlike the foxes and the birds, had no where to lay his head. Not that Jesus had no home to go to. Most people would be delighted to have the rabbi as their guest. It means that he was not sure where his next dwelling place would be when he was on a teaching or preaching trip. He traveled from village to village and the open countryside became his classroom. No wonder his most profound teachings were taught in parables. Parables are metaphors skillfully crafted in story form. Jesus was a master teacher in the use of parables. He talked about the sower and his seed when he passed by a field. Along the way he met shepherds with their sheep, workers laboring in a vineyard, guests enjoying a wedding feast, and fishermen casting their nets. All these encounters served as metaphors in his teachings about

---

2. Phillips, *The Cultivated Life*, 40.

the Kingdom of God. The disciples' classroom and learning experience was formed through walking with Jesus.

A good example is the story of Jesus walking with the two disciples on the road to the village of Emmaus. The two disciples journeyed with a heavy heart because of the sad news that a prophet of God, powerful in word and deed, was killed in Jerusalem. They had high hopes on him to redeem Israel. Their hopes were dashed when news of his death reached them. To add to the confusion, there were rumors that the prophet's body disappeared. Some women even saw angels who told them that Jesus was alive. Dejected and confused, they entered into a deep discussion over what had taken place. Jesus drew alongside and walked with them. He explained to them how such things were already predicted long ago in the Scriptures. They invited Jesus to eat with them in their home when they reached the village. Their confused minds suddenly recognized Jesus as the Savior when he broke bread with them. The two disciples, upon reflection, were surprised to find their hearts strangely warmed when Jesus talked to them on the road.

## The Simple Act of Walking

Walking was the primary mode of transport in Jesus' time. It still is today. Not all of us have cars or hoverboards to carry us, but all of us have two legs and a pair of eyes. With these, we are sufficiently equipped to walk properly. Walking involves the simple act of putting one foot before the other. We do not need skills or equipment to walk. Space is not a restriction when we walk. We are free to chart our own paths and to determine the length and duration of the journey. Time is not a restriction too. Some prefer morning walks while others like to walk at night. There are others who love walking under the hot sun or in the falling rain. I live in cities all my life. It is very rare for me to enjoy walking in the countryside at night. Twice I walked under a full moon in the countryside. The entire landscape was flooded with moonlight because these places were dark and far away from artificial lighting. Once I walked through a vegetable farm in rural China while on my way to a nearby village to watch a cultural performance by the locals. The other time was when I walked on rocky terrain on my way to the top of a high treeless mountain. The two places were magical and surreal and the experience was unforgettable.

We walk all the time. We walk from one place to another. We walk from home to office, office to the local grocery store, local store to the nearby market or school, and school or market back to home. Walking, in this manner, is transitional and carries no value on its own.[3] It is merely an empty space in between two places. The space is an inconvenient hindrance and walking in this space is more of a chore. Hence, we always look for the shortest way to transit between these two points. We are not focusing on the journey when we leave our home for work. Rather, our minds are absorbed with the events that we left behind at home and the things that will need our attention at the workplace. Likewise, when we leave work for home, we may want to detour and make a quick dash to the store for some domestic supplies. While walking, our minds are running through the list of things we want to purchase for the evening's dinner.

## The Extended Walk

An extended walk is different. The walk is not merely to transit between two points. The walk itself carries a value on its own. The inverse happens in this manner of walk.[4] Instead of the walk being disruptive and an inconvenience, the places at both ends of the journey become transitional points. The landscape along the way takes on an element of familiarity, stability, and permanence. Unlike the former, where the home, school, market or store are familiar places to us with familiar faces, each home or lodging along the extended walk looks different from the previous one. We never sleep on the same bed twice, the hosts are strangers to us, the decor and ambiance differ from place to place.

---

3. Gros, *A Philosophy of Walking*, 31.
4. Ibid., 32.

# THE METAPHOR OF WALKING

We were prepared for all kinds of sleeping arrangements when we were walking the mountain trails in Nepal. We cared little for the place, decor, or even the food we eat. The menu, offered to the guests in most lodgings or tea houses, was more or less the same with standardized prices. After a while of experimenting with various choices, ranging from Western to Asian dishes, we decided to stick to the basic Nepali dish which was a mixture of rice and lentil soup. It was a national dish and most Nepalis would take *Dal Baht* at least twice a day. It was relatively affordable and sufficient to fill our empty stomachs. The carbohydrates we consumed should be able to provide enough fuel for us to last another leg of our journey. The food prices were not cheap by Nepali standards. Conversely, the room rates were surprisingly affordable. All we wanted was a place to rest our tired bodies. While resting we planned for the journey ahead of us . With enough sleep, we should be ready for the next day's walk on the trail. A strange and exciting feeling ran through us as we began our day's walk. The outside landscape, with its fresh air, great sights, and the beautiful people we met on the way, was where we belonged. The inside lodgings were stopover places where we could rest our tired feet and bodies. Refreshed the next morning, we could be on our way to the next destination wherever that might be.

## States of Well-being Generated by Walking

The benefits of walking are well known to us. Walking increases the heart beat, opens the sweat pores, clears the head and lungs, strengthens the muscles, keeps our body in good shape, and opens our eyes to the sights that we usually miss seeing while driving or cycling. We know that walking reduces stress and gives us a sense of well-being when it releases endorphins in the body. When the body's muscles run out of stored oxygen, they produce lactic acid. This in turn triggers the brain to release endorphins that help to ease the pain and stress in the body. At the same time, the body enjoys a sensation of pleasure and euphoria.

## Take Up Your Mat and Walk

According to a study published recently by the National Academy of Sciences, a 90 minute walk reduces the levels of obsessive worry. It reduces the flow of blood to the subgenual prefrontal cortex. Bad moods are caused by the increased blood flow to this part of the brain. Walking or hiking in the natural environment tends to reduce its flow.[5] Frederic Gros in *A Philosophy of Walking* notes that the walking can lead us to experience different states of well-being in different degrees and on different occasions.[6] According to Gros, the different states of well-being generated by walking are pleasure, joy, happiness, and serenity.

I can identify with the different states of well-being described by Gros while walking the mountain trails in Nepal. For instance we encountered moments of pleasure along the way. The sudden discovery of a flowing stream of cool water, after a long and tiring walk, was such a moment. Before we reached the stream, the walk was especially difficult because of the steep slopes leading to the ravine below. Soaking our tired and bruised feet in the cool running water was pure pleasure. I even put a bottle of *Mountain Dew* in the running water to cool it.

Arriving at a tea-house after a long and tedious walk brought joy to our hearts. Laying aside our backpacks, stretching and resting our feet, sipping milk tea, and soaking in the sights and sounds of the pristine surroundings was a joyful experience seldom encountered in the busyness of urban life. The joy of having arrived and taking shelter at our lodge after a hard day's walk or looking back and see how far we had progressed since the last stop gave us a sense of accomplishment and satisfaction. A sense of fullness sank in. The same feeling of joy flooded our soul and body when we reached the summit, 3210 meters above sea level, at Poon Hill. We trekked from the village of Ghorepani at five in the early morning in order to catch the sunrise at the summit. The wind was freezing cold but we were not deterred by the elements. Fortunately, hot coffee, tea or chocolate were available at the summit though the price was a bit steep.

5. Pirrone, "What Hiking Does to the Brain is Pretty Amazing."
6. Gros, *A philosophy of Walking*, 140–46.

# THE METAPHOR OF WALKING

A happy state of well-being was when we woke up way before dawn to greet the rising sun over the Himalayan range. We needed to be early. We would not want to miss the opportunity to watch the beams of sunlight creeping slowly over the vast horizon. A group of us from different nationalities were standing in the cold air waiting with anticipation. Cupping our hands around mugs of hot coffee just to catch the first glimpse of dawn was worth the waiting and patience. The anticipated moment was magical. Our faces broke into happy smiles at the first rays of the sun streaking pins of light over the shadowed mountains. Having shared this special moment, we departed to our various places happy to know that we had received and participated in nature's blessings and glory.

Unlike running, cycling or driving, walking makes slow progress. We cannot push ourselves too hard because we have a long way to go. We need to conserve the body's energy to last the day's journey. Neither do we lag behind or else we will not be able to complete this leg of our journey. We walk at our own pace. We keep our legs moving in rhythmic fashion, and not thinking much about anything else but walk. Just walk. Walking in this manner will free our minds from the daily grind of fears and hopes. Our minds are no longer troubled by unfinished tasks and anticipated anxieties. A sense of serenity sets in as we walk. With this state of mind, it is easier for us to make friends on the trail. Most of the people we meet are complete strangers to us. It is not an uncommon sight to see people from different nationalities sitting together around a warm fireplace sharing notes and trading interesting stories in the evening.

## Value to the Soul

Walking that generates these states of well-being is more than a physical activity. It has value to our soul and spirit. It is not unusual for some people to treat walking as a spiritual discipline. John Muir, author and environmentalist, wrote that when he went out for a walk in the High Sierras, he was led to stay put until sundown because "for going out, I found, was really going in."[7] I had this experience when I visited the Temple of Heaven in Beijing. The place had a large forested area surrounding the buildings. The iconic building was an attraction, but I spent most of the morning walking the paths that crisscrossed the forested area. The place was not crowded with people. Most of the time I was alone. I lingered for a long time in this place because I felt a spiritual connection with it. Belden Lane, writer and professor, explains why wilderness hiking can be a form of spiritual discipline. When he goes hiking into the wilderness, he is not looking to exercise or to escape. He goes hiking to experience a depth of physical and spiritual intimacy. He writes:

> I'm moved by nature's power and beauty, but what sets me afire is the longing I sense there of everything else wanting to connect, the desire for an intimacy that is as alluring as it is frightening. I go to spend time alone with God . . . in a robust and full-bodied way.[8]

## Walking As Metaphor

In this book, I will use the metaphor of walking to explore and explain the various aspects of the spiritual life. For example, I will explain why the journey motif is important to our spiritual lives. I will also look into the need to engage our body in our spiritual growth. The need for presence, space, wonder, solitude, and freedom of simplicity in our spiritual lives will also be highlighted and discussed. Metaphorical language is used widely in Scripture. Metaphors have the ability to carry over or across something known and familiar to something unknown and unfamiliar. It acts as a bridge between the visible and the invisible. Since we are are primed to think and feel metaphorically, it is easier to communicate using metaphors to make sense of the visible and invisible world around us. Metaphors, though not intimidating and non

---

7. Muir, *My First Summer in the Sierra*, 75.
8. Lane, *Backpacking with the Saints*, 10.

confrontational, if used correctly can also be pervasive and influential. They also have the ability to induce us to participate and get involved in the matters of the soul. Parker Palmer, educator and activist, writes:

> If soul truth is to be spoken and heard, it must be approach "on a slant" . . . But soul truth is so powerful that we must allow ourselves to approach it, and it to approach us indirectly. We must invite, not command, the soul to speak. We must allow, not force, ourselves to listen.[9]

## The Call to Journey

Chapter 2 deals with the journey motif that is often used in Scriptures to describe the Christian life. Walking was the most common mode of transport in biblical times. Jesus invites us to walk with him on a journey. The people of God, metaphorically speaking, are always on the move. They are, biblically speaking, pilgrims and strangers in this world. Abraham was called to journey to an unknown future based on a promise given by God (Gen 12:1). He sojourned as an alien in a foreign land by making a radical break with the past. Abraham never owned the land that God promised him. Instead he lived a life of trust and obedience as he journeyed on. Israel, under Moses, spent a full generation of forty years journeying in the wilderness. He even named his son *Gershom*[10] for he had become an alien in a foreign land (Exod 2:22). Jesus, in the Gospels, journeyed to many places across Galilee, Judah, and beyond as an itinerant preacher teaching to attentive crowds. We know that the book of Acts is structured around the missionary journeys of Paul. We detect a sojourning theology in the epistles of Paul. He cautions us not to entangle ourselves with earthly matters for our citizenship is in heaven (Phil 3:19–20).

---

9. Palmer, *A Hidden Wholeness*, 92.
10. It means "an alien there."

# Take Up Your Mat and Walk

## Engaging the Body

Chapter 3 highlights the need to engage our physical bodies in our spirituality. Our bodies are engaged when we walk. It is impossible to ignore our physical bodies. This morning I went walking up a hill. I went up a path that winded its way through a forest of trees before I hit a road that led to my destination. It was a good walk but much energy was spent making the way to the stop point. I can feel the ache in my legs and feet while I am writing this chapter. It is easy to ignore the body when we think of spiritual matters. This has to do with our dualistic worldview that was informed and shaped by Greek philosophy. The Greeks believed that the material was inferior to the spiritual. The body should be suppressed or ignored in the spiritual life. Listen to what the psalmist has to say about engaging the body: "My soul thirsts for you, my body longs for you, in a dry and weary land where there was no water . . . my heart and my flesh cry out for the living God . . . my mouth will speak in praise of the Lord (Ps 63:1; 84:2; 145:21). Paul urges us to present our bodies as living sacrifices which is our spiritual act of worship (Rom 12:1). He hopes that while in prison he will not be ashamed but will have sufficient courage so that "Christ will be exalted in my body, whether by or by death (Phil 1:20). It is foolish not to engage our bodies in nurturing our spiritual lives since every spiritual discipline we undertake requires the use of the body. "The body," as Belden Lane explains, "plays a major role in authentic soul work. Any radical separation of body and soul makes the spiritual life impossible."[11]

## Attuned to the Moment

We will look into the practice of being attuned to the present moment in chapter 4. When we walk we have to mind our steps. We need to pay attention to where we are going. There was a fellow hiker who momentarily stopped before descending a series of steps. I was right behind him waiting impatiently for my turn to

---

11. Lane, *Backpacking with the Saints*, 8.

descend. He spent a few moments surveying the rugged, uneven steps before he made his next move. He studied them carefully in order to navigate the descending steps safely. To be attentive to the present moment is an important virtue needful to cultivate the spiritual life. Conversely, inattentiveness is to allow our minds to focus on what has gone before or what may be or ought to be. The steady walk and the heavy breathing, in a repetitive mode, produce a trance-like experience. In this way walking can be a form of meditation. We find ourselves alive to the things around us.[12] Our senses become attuned to the surrounding environment after a long walk. We become more aware of the local flora and fauna that line the trail, the sound of running water from a nearby stream, the noise made by insects and unseen animals in the forest, the movements of leaves and branches caused by the wind, the rugged terrain that lay before us, the faces of people we meet on the trail, and even the change in weather conditions. In our walk we take time to notice the details of the wonderful world that we often miss while we are in our hurry to somewhere. Our bodies are so attuned to the landscape that we are more aware of our feet pounding the ground below after days and weeks of walking. We feel an intimate connection with the landscape as we navigate our way through it.

## A Sense of Wonder

Chapter 5 stresses on the need to cultivate a sense of wonder in life. God uses two texts to reveal himself to us: the book of the Word and the book of Nature. The book of Nature is where God speaks to us through his handiwork (Ps 19:2). Augustine, the bishop of Hippo, believes that these two books can change lives: "We know of no other books with the like power to lay pride low and so surely to silence the obstinate contender."[13] Walking is the best way for us to "read" the book of Nature. When we walk we are greeted by nature that constantly begs for our attention. We need to develop a sense of wonder in order to read well. Wonder leads us to see the

---

12. Ibid., 100.
13. Augustine, *Confessions* XIII, 17. Cited by Lane, 25.

world as mysterious and sacred. While science seeks answers from nature, wonder responds to the mystery of life without the need for answers. Wonder does not impose on its object but let it speaks its own voice. All we need is to be open and attentive to the things around us. Unfortunately, our capacity to wonder has diminished in a rational world ruled by science and technology. Growing up, we lose the childlike wonder. A child can play for hours with simple toys made of material provided by nature. Adults need more sophisticated and expensive toys to keep their enthusiasm alive. No wonder Jesus told his disciples to become like little children in order to enter the kingdom of heaven (Matt 18:3).

## An Inner Space

We will look into the need to create an inner space in our spiritual lives in chapter 6. A Taoist saying goes like this: "Feet on the ground occupy very little space; it's through all the space they don't occupy that we can walk."[14] This saying reminds us that standing still in one place and not moving about is not an easy thing to do. Standing occupies very little space and is restrictive. We feel uneasy if we stand for too long unless we are occupied with some work, game or entertainment. This is the reason why standing in one corner and not doing anything is often used as a form of punishment for a child who misbehaves. Standing still requires effort and discipline. It is strange to say this but it is true. Our feet are made more to walk than to stand still. Walking helps our feet find balance and rhythm. Our feet measure distance and occupy space when we walk. Walking makes us aware of the open space before us. This open space outside of us has an impact on the inner space inside us.

Kathleen Norris, poet and cultural critic, moved from New York city to a rural village in northwestern South Dakota. Her experiences in this small rural town led her to write *Dakota: A Spiritual Geography*. Unlike New York which was overshadowed by tall skyscrapers, the small town of just over a thousand residents was

14. Gros, *A Philosophy of Walking*, 185.

dominated by vast tracts of land and sky. Staying in Dakota helped her to make this observation; she noticed that a person was forced inward by the sparseness of what was outward and visible in all this land and sky.[15] To develop a space in our hearts for God and neighbors is necessary and vital to our spiritual life. Neighborliness and friendship are spiritual fruits that we hope to cultivate. It is observed, and I think it is true, that people who live in less crowded areas, with open spaces dominated by land and sky, tend to be more hospitable and trusting than those who live in crowded urban areas overshadowed by high buildings.

## A Solitary Walk

Chapter 7 highlights the need for solitude in our spiritual lives. A walker, if she has a choice, usually walks alone. Not that she does not like company. To walk well she needs to find her own rhythm and maintain the pace throughout. In this way, walking is at its optimal level. If she has to follow someone's pace, either slower or faster, she may not walk that well. This will disturb her rhythm and pace. Hence, the walker must get use to the idea of being alone most of the time.[16] The solitary walk not only helps us to reflect and meditate, but it is essential to our spiritual lives as well. Solitude keeps us in touch with our true selves. We easily forget who we are if we do not find time to be alone. Away from the expectations of the crowd, our identities are no longer forged by externalities. Instead, our identities are forged by God who dwells in us. We no longer need to market ourselves based on how well we perform before others. During these solitary walks we begin to discover our authentic selves and gain a deeper understanding of who God is in our life. Shielded from the distractions of the world by solitude we are more open and awaken to the inner workings of God in us. We talk less and listen more. We can be present to our selves and neighbor. This will help us to be a more compassionate person.

---

15. Norris, *Dakota: A Spiritual Geography*, 157.
16. Gros, *A Philosophy of Walking*, 53.

## The Simple Life

The last chapter deals with the freedom of simplicity the soul enjoys. Walking will teach us to detach from the things that bother us on a daily basis. Our minds become less cluttered with worries, possessions, and image building. We leave behind the daily exchanges of work, goods, and information that serve our egos. These are no longer significant. Those things that we take for granted like bread to fill our stomach, water to quench our thirst, a hat or shade to shield us from the sun or rain, and a walking stick are greatly appreciated for those who walk the trail. We do not need to carry a lot of stuff on the trail. The bare essentials are sufficient to make the trip a delightful one. This detachment or indifference is liberating and frees us from getting entangled with the mundane things of consumerism. Modern life defines people in terms of how much they have accumulated or consumed. The freedom of simplicity we assume is counter-cultural and is important to our spiritual life. Christianity is counter-cultural. We are not to conform to this world but be transformed by having the mind of Christ.

## Crossing the Threshold

A journey begins with the first step. This first step is crucial and for some of us this is the threshold that launches us to an amazing journey with God. Some of us are reluctant to cross this threshold. This threshold prevents us from taking the first step. It draws the line between the familiar and the unknown, the past and the future. It means letting God lead us to unknown, untested, and sacred territory. This journey is different from taking a vacation. Everything are worked out in advance for our comfort and convenience when we are on holiday. We are briefed on the itinerary and we know what to expect for our trip. We will harbor no surprises. The spiritual journey is more like a pilgrimage. Like all pilgrims we are required to make sacrifices and are not looking for comfort or having a good time. We will meet with surprises along the way.

## THE METAPHOR OF WALKING

Our faith will be tried and tested. We will face resistance and obstacles as we make progress in our journey. The pilgrim journeys on because he longs to connect and encounter the sacred. He is willing to overcome fear and pain in order to be in touch with the divine and be transformed. Only then will he find his life enriched with meaning, purpose, and challenges.

The word "threshold"comes from the word "threshing". Usually threshing is done at the door step of farm houses to separate the grains from the husks. The first step is the step of renewal that separates the old from the new. It is a journey filled with risk but with great potential for a spiritually enriched life. To live an enriched life, a walker learns how to make the most of his journey with God. He learns the importance of engaging his physical body and letting it be the means to develop his spiritual disciplines. There is no separation between soul and body. An authentic spiritual life requires the help of the body for its growth and development. Taking care of the health of our bodies is part of our spiritual exercises. The hurried life is not good for our souls. Practicing the art of mindfulness or to be present to the moment will help us to slow down. Slowing down will lead us to be open to the presence of God around us. As a walker we also need to develop a sense of wonder. Wonder is necessary to our spiritual life because without it we will not be open to the mysteries around us. Wonder helps us to see the fingerprints of God in and around us. The ordinary, permeated by the divine, can be only perceived through wonder.

An inner space in our hearts is formed when we are exposed to the outer space in our walk. We need room in our hearts for God and neighbor. This act of hospitality is an expression of love to ourselves, God, and others. The chief outcome of a enriched spiritual life is love. Only the true self can give love. The practice of solitude will lead to the emergence of the true self. It is easy to forget who we are when we are part of a crowd. When we are alone we begin to discover who we truly are. It frees us from wanting acclaim and approval from others. Without solitude, our sense of self is nurtured by our cravings for security, control, and affection. The enriched life is also a simple life. The simple life frees us from the snares of consumerism. It is to seek God's kingdom first and to live life from the Center. The competing selves pull us in different directions and our lives become complicated. Living an integrated life helps us not only to achieve inner simplicity but outward simplicity as well.

## Questions for Reflection and Discussion

1. Why is it difficult for some people to cross the "threshold" and begin walking with Jesus? What difficulties do you face when you come across a "threshold" in your life?
2. What are required of you to walk with Jesus?
3. What are the difficulties you think you will face when you seriously take up the challenge to walk with Jesus?
4. How can you make walking a part of your spiritual practice?

*Chapter 2*

# THE CALL TO JOURNEY

> Not a day goes by when the world doesn't cry out for us, signal us with signs and sounds, calling us home.
>
> —PHIL COUSINEAU[1]

ONE DAY A MAN was invited by his king to dine with him in his castle.[2] He was thrilled knowing that it was indeed an honor to meet the king. At the same time, he was anxious about the long journey to the king's castle. There were many paths to the king's castle but he wasn't sure which was the right one. The day came when he had no choice but to face the journey. The man was a carpenter by trade. Along the way he decided to spend the night. So he built a simple shelter. When he was about to leave the next morning, he looked back and realized that he could built a better shelter. So he decided to delay the journey and began work on improving the shelter. He spent a long time upgrading his shelter. With time, the shelter began to take shape and more things were added to it. Before long, the shelter became a proper house with many added amenities. The poor man had forgotten about the journey to dine with the king at his castle while busily building his house.

---

1. Cousineau, *The Art of Pilgrimage*, 39.
2. Story adapted from Griebner, "The Carpentar and the Unbuilder" 24–25.

## The Awakened Soul

Jesus, our King, has invited us to go on a journey. I remember saying that Christians ought to be walkers but many prefer to live the sedentary lifestyle that inhibits the spiritual life. We are not on a journey because we are so engrossed in making a living that we have forgotten how to live. We are so rooted in our present lives that we have forgotten where our true home is. Many of us are spiritually in deep slumber. We will not begin to travel on life's most important journey unless we are awakened by the deep longing that God has implanted in our souls. This inward journey may be the longest journey we will take during our lifetime. This desire, at the very core of our souls, is dampened and crowded out by other fleshly desires that beg for our attention. Once a while, we may sense this awakening in our souls but it fades away just as quickly as it comes. This opportune moment, like the Greek god *Kairos* with winged feet and scepter, is sweeping past us as quickly as it comes. "When a moment knocks on the door of our life," wrote Russian novelist Boris Pasternak, "it is often no louder than the beating of your heart, and it is very easy to miss it."[3]

Simone Weil gives an example of what a real awakening looks like.[4] It is like walking down a misty road at dusk. We see a stooping man through the mist, but when we draw near we begin to realize that it is not a man but a tree. It is like the scales over our eyes falling down and we are able to see things differently for the first time. This awakening happened to Paul on the Damascus road. He was bent on giving the Christians a hard time. That was his religious vocation and he was good at it. Paul saw things differently after the Damascus road experience. A voice asked Paul, "Saul, Saul, why are you persecuting me?" Paul realized that he was not fighting against the Christians but he was fighting against Jesus instead.

A young Jew once approached a well known Jewish teacher. He asked the rabbi saying, "Rebbe, what is the way to God?" The

---

3. Cited by Cousineau, *The Art of Pilgrimage*, 37.
4. Kidd, *God's Joyful Surprise*, 150.

## THE CALL TO JOURNEY

rabbi looked up from his work and replied, "There is no way to God, for God is not other than here and now. The truth you seek is not hidden from you; you simply do not notice it. It is here for you if you will only awake."[5] God is closer to us that we can ever imagine. God is not far from each of us for "in him we live and move and have our being" (Acts 17:27-28). We mortals exist by using our breath. We breath in and we breath out. God is as close to us as our breathing. We hardly notice him because we are not awakened yet.

Dante was a political exile from Florence. He knew that he would never go back to his beloved hometown. Still, the heart's longing for home stayed with Dante all his life. Inspired by this, he wrote the *Divine Comedy*. It was a composition of three books of poems about a pilgrim's journey. In this journey he went down to the inferno of hell and up on the mountain of purgatory before he reached paradise, his true home. It began when he was awakened from his deep sleep. He found himself lost in a dark wood and realized that he had strayed from the straight path. This frightening discovery gave him the resolve to begin his journey to paradise. Like Paul and Dante, this awakening will set us on a journey that will change and transform our lives in a totally new way.

God uses different means to wake us from our spiritual slumber (Eph 5:14). David Benner's *Spirituality and the Awakening Self* highlights several invitations to awakenings that can propel us to take the journey.[6] The invitations can come from the circumstances of life: a nasty divorce, financial failure, vocational disillusionment, loss due to death or accidents. We hear testimonies of Christians who, after a period of difficulty and severe struggle, begin to take their faith and walk with God more seriously. Psychological symptoms like depression, anxiety, uncontrolled anger, and irritation can also be potential awakenings. Sometimes, as in the case of Paul, the outward circumstances and the inward struggles combined to awaken and propel him on a journey with God that bored great consequences for the Christian church. The

---

5. Benner, *Spirituality and the Awakening Self*, 1.
6. Ibid, 7-9.

sudden appearance of blinding light and voice coupled with the inner struggle of a guilty conscience (later Paul called himself the chief of sinners) led him to change the course of his life. When reprimanded on the Damascus road by Jesus, Paul did not defend himself, protest or turn abusive. Rather, out of a guilty conscience, he spent the time fasting and reflecting over the incident before he made his next move based on God's directive.

## We Learn As We Journey

It is good to know that the journey we take is not just transiting between two points. In normal circumstances, when we leave a place for another, we reflect on the events that we leave behind or anticipating the things that need our attention at our destined place. We seldom think much of the journey because it is transient. The spiritual journey is different. The spiritual journey is rooted in the present. The Gospel of Mark is structured around a journey motif (8:22–10:52). This is clearly detected in the use of the phrase "on the way" several times in this section:

> Jesus and his disciples went on to the villages around Caesarea Phillippi. On the way he asked them, "Who do people say I am?" (Mark 8:27).
>
> As Jesus started on his way, a man ran up to him and fell on his knees before him, "Good teacher," he asked, "what must I do to inherit eternal life?" (Mark 10:17).
>
> They were on the way to Jerusalem, with Jesus leading the way, and the disciples were astonished, while those who followed were afraid (Mark 10:32).

This part of the Gospel is also the discipleship section of Mark. The disciples learned as they journeyed with Jesus. Jesus, on the way to Jerusalem, made full use of this time to teach his followers knowing that his days were numbered. While passing through Galilee, he did not want the crowds to know where they were so that he could use this time to teach the disciples privately (9:30). He knew that he would face death when he arrived at Jerusalem

(8:31). The cross was waiting for him. Jesus decided to stay focus on the journey and not deterred by the tribulation that awaited him in Jerusalem.

## The Difficulties of Learning

Knowledge of self and God is essential to our spiritual life. When we walk with Jesus on the way we begin to discover who we are through our struggles and who God is in terms of what he is doing in our life. This does not mean that everything go on smoothly as planned. The spiritual journey has its ups and downs. It has its ambiguities, difficulties, and frustrations as well as periods of growth in self-understanding, increased presence of God, and a heart filled with compassion.[7]

Peter is a good example (Mark 8:29, 31–33; 9:2–6). On the way he gained a deeper understanding of himself and of God. This knowledge did not come easy for Peter. He stumbled all the way. He testified that Jesus was the Christ, the Messiah. This was indeed a revelation. His understanding, on the other hand, was filled with ambiguity. He misunderstood the messianic role of Jesus and his mission. He received a stinging rebuke when he cautioned Jesus for talking about his coming death. He even had a bigger surprise when Jesus transfigured before him in the presence of two saints that he admired: Moses and Elijah. Peter was so enthused by this mountaintop sensation that he loved to stay longer. He suggested building shelters for Jesus and the two important guests. Again Peter misread the incident for Mark wrote that he, our of fear at this dramatic event, did not know what to say. Maybe it was fear plus ignorance. At this stage of the journey, Peter had not learned the cost of discipleship. He had not learned that following Jesus the Messiah meant denying self and taking up his own cross. Not wanting Jesus to face death revealed his own self interest. Jesus' death meant that he gained nothing by following him. On the mountain, Peter's suggestion to build the shelters clearly showed his heart's

---

7. Chase, *The Tree of Life*, 136.

desire. He wanted to enjoy the blissful moment without giving a second thought about the significance of Jesus' transfiguration.

It is interesting to take note that this discipleship section in the Gospel of Mark is framed by two stories of blind men who were healed by Jesus. These two healing stories are vastly different from each other (Mark 8:22–26; 10:46–52). The second healing of blind Bartimaeus, as expected, was immediate. Conversely, the first healing was a two-staged affair. When Jesus first touched the man's eyes he could only see partially. He saw people like trees walking around. In other words, his vision was still blurred and not sharp. He was able to see clearly when Jesus touched him the second time. Why must Jesus took the trouble to heal him twice instead of once? In all his healing miracles, Jesus word was sufficient. He didn't need to touch the person. It was not that he lacked the power to heal instantly. Sight is used as a metaphor for understanding. We often use the phrase, "I see" to show that we understand whatever has been communicated to us.

This two staged healing by Jesus showed that the understanding of the disciples toward the mission of Jesus was incomplete, only partial. They had a hard time figuring out why Jesus had to suffer, die, and rise again after three days. They had not grasped the full implications of what it took to follow Jesus and why discipleship had to be costly. On the way, James and John even asked to sit on the left and right side of Jesus in his glory. The disciples knew that the person who sat in these places held positions of power and honor. Earlier they were arguing about who was the greatest. No wonder the other disciples were indignant at James and John for their selfish ambitions.

## Learning the Language of Paradox

The disciples' understanding of discipleship was shallow. They had a lot to learn. Jesus was patient with them. According to Jesus, one must learn to serve in order to lead well. To be first, one must learn to be the very last. This was not only hard for the disciples but difficult for us to swallow as well. These self-contradictory statements sound absurd and counter-cultural. We need to adopt the language of paradox if we want to learn as we journey with Jesus.[8] Our journey with Jesus will take us to new experiences in terms of the people and places we encounter on the way. We know that the greatest barrier, while in a foreign land, is to speak the local language. We feel lost and helpless if we cannot master the language. Likewise, journeying in God's kingdom requires us to pick up the language of paradox. We need humility and a submissive spirit to learn for the language of paradox goes against our instinct for dominance and survival.

Earlier, the disciples were challenged to deny self and take up the cross to follow Jesus (Mark 8:34). The cross itself is paradoxical. Nothing about the cross makes sense. It doesn't make sense for an innocent man to die a death reserved only for criminals. It doesn't make sense for a sinless person to bear the sins on our behalf. It doesn't make sense for a man to love and forgive his enemies. Judy Cannato rightly observes that we need to live with the language of paradox though we cannot resolve it. It is the language of the spiritually mature. Like most languages, we need to put in time and effort to learn and master it.[9]

## Different Stages of Growth

Discipleship can be misunderstood if we view spirituality as something we can acquire in terms of information or techniques.[10] It is easy for us, in a do-it-yourself culture, to be drawn to this misconceived idea of following Jesus. We have this wrong notion that with the right programs and methodology, we should be able to find spiritual fulfillment. In this way, we are in control of our spiritual life and our relationship with God is shaped by "doing" rather than "being". Most of the spirituality we observe nowadays is based on this misconception. This kind of spirituality usually follows the latest trends and will not last. Conversely, we can view our spirituality as a journey. Our role in this journey is to respond to the one who

---

8. Cannato, "Paradox Road" 39–40.
9. Ibid, 40–41.
10. Mulholland, *Invitation to a Journey*, 12.

leads. God is in control and he is the one "whose purpose shapes our path, whose grace redeems our detours, whose power liberates us from crippling bondages of the prior journey and whose transforming presence meets us at each turn of the road."[11]

The aim of the journey is to be like Jesus. When we follow Jesus and learn to submit to his ways, we become more and more like the master. It is Paul's prayer for the Ephesians, and our prayers too, that we "may be filled to the measure of all the fullness of God" (3:19). Paul further says that "we all reach unity in the faith and in the knowledge of the Son of God and become mature, attaining to the whole measure of the fullness of Christ" (4:13). We become more Christlike when our relationship and love with God deepen. Hence, the spiritual life is more than just actively doing God's work, adhering to a prescribed moral or ethical code, and subscribing to a set of belief or doctrines. The spiritual life requires us to engage God in every area of our lives on a daily basis.

We know that healthy growth comes in stages. The biblical model of spiritual growth is mentioned by the apostle John. He describes spiritual growth in terms of the three distinct stages of faith: children, young men, and fathers (1 John 2:12–14). These stages of growth are not age-related and have to be viewed metaphorically revealing different levels of maturity. The childhood stage refers to the newborn in Christ who strive to develop a new spiritual identity based on the love of the Father. The young men are those who, having grounded themselves in God's Word, have the strength to live out their faith victoriously in the world dominated by the flesh and the devil. The fathers are those who have developed and enjoyed a ripe faith and, through their godly examples, are empowering others to grow to spiritual maturity.

The classical model of spiritual growth has three stages: purgation, illumination, and union.[12] Based on the model by the apostle John, these three stages or ways were later advanced by the church authorities. The purgative way includes conversion to Christ, the renunciation of sins, the practice of spiritual disci-

---

11. Ibid., 12.
12. Demarest, "Reflections on Developmental Spirituality" 154.

plines, and a gradual detachment to the material life in order to pay more attention to the spiritual life. The illuminative way enters a new phase in spiritual growth. A profound transformation takes place where God is taking control of the spiritual relationship. A greater consecration and deepening of God's love takes place in the believer's life characterized by virtues of humility, self-control, and patience. At this stage, prayer becomes less discursive and more contemplative. The unitive way as pointed out by Jesus in John 14:20 as "you in me and I in you" is the highest stage. Many believers may not be able to reach this stage of spiritual maturity. This stage is reserved for those whose life is characterized by contemplative prayers, the dark nights, and ecstatic union. Pseudo-Macarius, the forth century theologian, described the three stages of the journey as progressing "from the heart possessed by evil, to a heart indwelt by sin and grace, and then ultimately to a heart that belongs to God alone."[13]

## The Dark Night of the Soul

Someone says that when we walk with God, we are always arriving and never arrive. A person who journeys with God can never say that her task on earth is finished. There will always be something new for her to learn. When God has transformed one area of her life, new areas pop up that require her attention. The journey is never a smooth ride. It is filled with difficulties, frustrations, challenges, blessings, hope, and joy. There are times when we are tempted to turn back or quit walking the path altogether. We find ourselves stagnating spiritually and things are not working out well for us. We wonder what is wrong with us. Nothing seems to excite us anymore. We have lost the passion and joy for spiritual matters. At this point in our journey we may have entered a period called the "dark night of the soul" that John of the Cross wrote about some five hundred years ago. Most of us may not even know what is this "dark night". We know that we have entered into the

---

13. Ibid., 155.

"dark night" when we feel that God has abandoned us and left us to fend for ourselves.

> Our good feelings of God's presence evaporate. We feel the door to heaven has been shut as we pray. Darkness, helplessness, weariness, a sense of failure or defeat, barrenness, emptiness, dryness descend upon us. The Christian disciplines that have served us up to this time "no longer work." We can't see what God is doing and we see little visible fruit in our lives.[14]

We should not be anxious if we know that God is using the dark night to do an even greater work in us. The dark night is a time of transition that God is using to usher us to a higher level of spiritual maturity. This is the time when we find ourselves confused, disorientated, and lost. Our role at this point is not to react fretfully but to be prayerful and wait for the time to pass us. We need to be patient for God to work at transforming our inner self. The work can be slow and takes time. The dark night is like the birth of a child. The child has to leave the warmth and security of the mother's womb by transiting through the dark birth canal before she exits into the bright world outside. Transitions are necessary for growth and progress. Transitions are opportune times when God is actively at work in our lives. When we come out of these times, we will find ourselves armed with a clearer understanding of who we are, with a greater appreciation of God's love for us, with a renewed confidence in our faith, and with a more sincere love for others. Having experienced brokenness through the dark night, we become less judgmental on others. We are more willing to trust God without knowing all the answers. Our capacity to wait on God has increased, and we feel the freedom to let go of those things that we deem are not important anymore.[15] We are now ready to serve him with a deeper love and greater commitment than before.

---

14. Scazzero, *Emotionally Healthy Spirituality*, 122–23.
15. Ibid., 127–32.

# THE CALL TO JOURNEY

## Awakened Desires Lead to a Changed Life

We begin this journey when we are awakened to the desire that is lodged deep in our soul. Until this time, our longing or thirst for God is crowded out by other desires that we wrongly perceive will define who we are. We look to our jobs, achievements, titles, status, and relationships for fulfillment but we are mostly disappointed. This desire, which is rooted in love, compels us to go on a quest. Most of the time we are not in touch with our deepest desire. Our memory fails us. But when we are awakened to this longing, we begin to recognize this holy desire as a gift of joy from God. This unspeakable joy draws us to God. To C. S. Lewis, joy is to love and be loved, and is not exactly pleasure or happiness. It can be sweet even though painful at times because it is placed in our hearts by God's grace.[16]

In *The Art of Pilgrimage* Phil Cousineau begins with this statement: "My travels were moving question marks." He continues saying that "inside every question is a quest trying to get out."[17] Questions are asked to bring out the desires in our heart. Jesus used questions to help others keep in touch with their desires. "What do you want me to do for you?" he called out to blind Bartimaeus.[18] It was obvious what the blind man wanted when he cried out to Jesus, "Son of David, have mercy on me!" He wanted to see and he told Jesus so. Besides healing his sight, Jesus wanted him to get in touch with his deepest need. His need for physical sight was obvious, but he had a deeper desire that he had probably forgotten or ignored. He needed to be awakened to the spiritual longing which was rooted in God's love. Only Jesus could meet this thirst and bring joy and satisfaction to his soul. Jesus was inviting him to go on a journey with him. Bartimaeus took up the offer. He followed Jesus along the road after receiving his sight (Mark 10:52).

---

16. Douglas, "C. S. Lewis and our Longing for Home" 9.
17. Cousineau, *The Art of Pilgrimage*, xx, 88.
18. Barton, *Sacred Rhythms*, 23–24.

# Take Up Your Mat and Walk
## The Story of Rabbi Eisik

A long time ago, in the village of Cracow lived an old rabbi named Eisik.[19] One night he had a dream. The dream told him to go on a journey to Prague. Prague was a long way from his home. In that city he would look out for a bridge that led to the royal castle. Underneath the bridge was hidden a treasure of gold that would change his live forever. Eisik was reluctant to go at first due to the long journey. He wasn't sure whether the dream was true. The same dream came to him again the following night. Then it happened again a third time. Eisik could not contain himself anymore. He had to make the trip to Prague.

When the rabbi found the bridge he was disappointed because there were soldiers guarding the bridge that led to the royal castle. He wandered helplessly not knowing what to do since he could not enter the bridge to look for the treasure. Rain began falling and he was getting restless. Finally he was stopped by the captain of the guard who looked suspiciously at him. He asked whether he had lost something. The old rabbi said that he had not lost anything. Instead, he had come a long way to look for something. He then related the dream to the captain. He shared with the captain about the gold hidden underneath the bridge.

The captain burst out laughing and rebuked the rabbi for believing in dreams. "What reasonable man takes them seriously?" he asked. "As a matter of fact, I heard a voice call out in an absurd dream just a few nights ago, urging me to take a long journey to Cracow and visit a rabbi named Eisik. The voice told me to look in the recess behind his stove where I would find a gold treasure." The captain warned the rabbi not to be gullible and be tempted by greed. He went back to his post. The rabbi went home and immediately searched behind the stove in his kitchen. To his surprise, he found the gold treasure that ended his poverty and changed his life forever.

---

19. Story adapted from Cousineau's *The Art of Pillgrimage*, 32–34.

# THE CALL TO JOURNEY

## In Touch with the Inmost Self

If this treasure is in our house why do we need to go on a long journey to discover it? In order to be in touch with our inner self we need to take heed to the call to go on a journey. Only then can we discover our authentic self - who we truly are. Knowing our real self will change our lives. This is the paradox of life. The desire to seek for the gold treasure came from the dream. This desire was hidden in the rabbi's life all this while. This desire in him was awakened by the dreams he had. It was this desire that led him on a journey to discover himself. Many of us have lost contact with our innermost self. For this reason we tend to look for answers outwardly. Often the answers lie within ourselves.

Rainer Maria Rilke gave this advice to a young man who asked him whether he should become a poet. Kappus, the young man, sought out Rilke with the question: "Is there a great poet waiting to be born in me or should I let that dream go?" Rilke did not answer the young man directly. Instead he gave him this advice:

> Nobody can counsel and help you, nobody. There is only one single way. Go into yourself. Search for the reason that bids you to write; find out whether it is spreading out its roots in the deepest places of your heart, acknowledge to yourself whether you would have to die if it were denied you to write. This above all—ask yourself in the stillest hour of your night: must I write? Delve into yourself for the deep answer.[20]

To discover our true selves we need to take a journey. It is an inner journey of the soul that has outward consequences. It leads to a changed life. We learn as we journey. The journey will not be smooth going. There will be ups and downs. As pilgrims on the road we are ready to face the challenges to our faith. We will encounter difficulties and mistakes along the way. We will grow as we learn through the good and bad times. We become more spiritually matured. We begin to develop a new identity as children loved

---

20. Rilke, *Letters to a Young Poet*, 18–19.

by the Father. We gain a new insight into God's Word. From it we draw strength and grace to face a hostile world that does not know our God. As we grow further we begin to bear the fruits of our ripen faith. By setting an example of godliness we are empowering younger Christians to follow the path we have taken.

One of the things we want them to learn from our mistakes is not to ignore our physical bodies in our spirituality. We make the mistake of separating the body from the soul. The body plays no part in impacting our spiritual life because we wrongly conceive that spiritual matters only concern the soul. The body is seen as an impediment to our spiritual walk with God. We view the body as having no value for the soul. So we take pains to suppress or ignore it as a way to improve our spiritual life. This is a common mistake among Christians. It is important to pay attention to two things before we go further on this subject. First, God in his plan decided to take residence in a human body. It would be a permanent feature for Christ. He would not shed his bodily form in glory. Second, we too will have a glorified body in heaven. Though our bodies will waste away at death, they will be renewed and rejuvenated when life returns back to us. We cannot ignore our bodies. They will be with us through eternity. The Word of God says that we are to honor God with our bodies (1 Cor 6:20).

## Questions for Reflection and Discussion

1. Can you recall a time when your soul was awakened to journey with God? What was the thing that triggered this awakening?
2. Why is the Christian life paradoxical? How do you normally deal with the paradoxes of the Christian life?
3. At what stage of growth do you think you are right now? What steps do you need to take to move to the next level of growth?
4. How has you life changed when you decided to take up this journey with Jesus?

*Chapter 3*

# AN EMBODIED SPIRITUALITY

> The body . . . plays a major role in authentic soul work. Any radical separation of body and soul makes the spiritual life impossible.
>
> — BELDEN LANE[1]

## The Body is Suppressed or Ignored

WE NEED TO TAKE care of our bodies while on a journey. Elijah felt depressed thinking that his work for the Lord had amounted to nothing. Jezebel was totally unmoved despite the victory against the Baal worshipers at Mount Carmel. The queen spearheaded the apostasy in Israel. Elijah fought hard to turn Israel back to God. He killed the queen's prophets and she threatened to take his life. He had to run away from that evil queen, Jezebel. On his way to Mount Horeb, the prophet sat under a broom tree at Beersheba, the southern most town of Judah. Dejected, he asked the Lord to take his life for he had no desire to live on. He felt that all his hard work had gone down the drain and he was the only person fighting for the Lord in Israel. The prophet, at this point, was emotionally and physically exhausted. He was not thinking clearly because fatigue overcame his body. He was so tired that he fell asleep. An angel came along to wake him up and

---

1. Lane, *Backpacking with the Saints*, 8.

to give him something to eat and drink. He did this a second time. Before leaving, he advised the prophet to be physically fit in order to complete the journey (1 Kgs 19:1–8).

Most of us, like the prophet, tend to neglect our bodies as we journey with God. This has to do with our dualistic worldview that is informed and shaped by Greek philosophy. This worldview believes that the spiritual side of us is more superior that the physical side. The physical body, in essence, is evil. Conversely the soul is spiritual and good. To Plato, the body is just to contain the soul. The soul will leave our bodies at the point of death. We do not see ourselves as being a soul but having a soul.[2] The early Christians found the teachings of Plato concerning the soul attractive. The Greek philosophers believed in a perfect and immutable Supreme Being and the immortality of the soul. To avoid the perception that the Christian faith was superstitious as claimed by others, Platonic philosophy was used as an apologetic tool to interpret faith to the outsiders. Eventually, this too influenced the Christians' own understanding of their faith.

## The Flesh is Weak

Meanwhile, Paul's comment that the flesh is weak does not help. The flesh or sinful nature, according to Paul, is in conflict with the Spirit and the flesh desires what is contrary to the Spirit (Gal 5:17). Jesus' calling on his disciples to watch and pray so as not to fall into temptation for the spirit is willing and the body is weak gives the impression that the body is an impediment to the soul. It is not a surprise that the role of the body in the spiritual life is either ignored or suppressed by Christians. Christians do not trust the body since the worldly culture worships the human body. They observe this in the sports, entertainment, and fashion industries. Successful sports personalities, good looking celebrities, and fashionable models with the perfect body shape are idolized and sought after by the secular masses. Some Christians are offended

---

2. Benner, *Soulful Spirituality*, 79.

by fellow believers who put too much attention on their appearance by what they put on their faces or wear on their bodies.

On the other hand, Scripture advocates the use of the body for spiritual purposes. The body is a temple of the Holy Spirit. Since the temple is the place where sacrifices are made, we are asked to offer our bodies as a living sacrifices, holy and pleasing to God (Rom 12:1). We are called to honor God with our bodies (1 Cor 6:20). If this is the case, the body cannot be bad or evil. The psalmist has a high regard for the body. In recalling the Creator's wonderful handiwork of the majestic cosmos, the psalmist notes his amazing work in shaping the human body: "For you created my inmost being; you knot me together in my mother's womb. I praise you because I am fearfully and wonderfully made; your works are wonderful, I know them full well" (Ps 139:14).

## The Body is Not the Flesh

The problem is that we tend to equate flesh with the body. Paul uses different Greek words for flesh (*sarx*) and body (*soma*). The New International Version translates flesh as *sinful nature* to distinguish it from the physical body. We are born with a fallen nature that predisposes our bodies to sin. The body is a vehicle or instrument used either by the flesh or the Spirit as instruments of wickedness or righteousness (Rom 6:13). Our bodies become a battleground either for sin to reign over us or for God to rule through his Holy Spirit. We are called, as Christians, to be "dead to sin but alive to God in Christ Jesus" (Rom 6:11–12).

It is not easy for the young believer to do this. This takes time. We have been raised and nurtured in an ungodly environment since the day we were born. It is tough to shed our sinful habits the moment we become a child of God. The old nature will drag us down even as we intend to walk with God. Paul can testify that the things he wants to do, he cannot carry out, and the things he doesn't want to do, he keeps doing. As we slowly learn to yield parts of our lives to God, old habits are gradually denied and new ones are being formed. Sin shall not have mastery over us since we are no longer under law but under grace. We shall be able to let

Christ reign in our hearts by the provision of God's abundant grace and his gift of righteousness (Rom 6:14; 5:17).

## The Body is Needed for Growth

Someone may ask that if we need God's grace to grow the spiritual life then why the need of the body? Aren't faith and grace sufficient for us to be Christlike? God needs our cooperation in spiritual formation. Paul calls on us to work out our salvation with fear and trembling (Phil 2:12). He will not do it for us if we are not willing. A well-informed action with good intention on our part are needed for transformation to take place. Nothing happens if we do not make an effort to grow spiritually. Dallas Willard, a philosopher of religion, thinks that the human agency in using the body is needed for growth:

> Without the body in its proper place, the pieces of the puzzle of new life in Christ do not realistically fit together, and the idea of really following him and becoming like him remains a practical impossibility.[3]

We cannot ignore the body in our spiritual life. The soul cannot be separated from the body. Christians tend to think that they do not need to involve the body in spiritual formation. Take for example, the healing of the body. The focus is on getting the body healed physically. The healing is an end in itself and no thought is given to the body as a means of deepening the relationship with God. Jesus healed the ten lepers and only one came back to him, praising God with a loud voice. Jesus was surprised that only one, a foreigner, came back to God and the rest, though healed, had forgotten to give glory to God (Luke 17:18).[4]

We are a soulish body and, at the same time, an embodied soul. A priest came to Meister Eckhart and said: "I wish that your soul were in my body." Replying, he said: "You would really be foolish. That would get you nowhere —it would accomplish as little as

---

3. Porter, "The Willardian Corpus" 252.
4. Edwards, *Living in the Presence*, 17.

## AN EMBODIED SPIRITUALITY

for your soul to be in my body. No soul can really do anything except through the body to which it is attached."[5] Our spirituality is an embodied spirituality because we can only experience God in our bodies. If we focus only on the spiritual part of us and neglect the body then we are alienated not only from God, but from our true self and the world.[6] The result is a legalistic self-righteousness with a strong tendency to self-control and discipline.[7]

Alienation of the body will give Christians the wrong impression that to be spiritual, a person must avoid pursuing pleasure, play, and leisure that the body normally enjoys. To indulge in these activities will lead to feelings of guilt. The spiritual life is driven more by guilt than love. In order to be spiritual, some believers think that they must punish their bodies through abstinence. Many years ago I met a radar technician in church. He was a leader and fervent in serving the Lord. His commitment to the Lord was without question. One time he gladly proclaimed that he was able to abstain having sex with his wife for long periods of time. His self-control and discipline to subjugate his body was a sign of spiritual maturity to him. He gave the impression that bodily desires if not subdued could lead him to sin against God.

### God took up residence in the Body

God, in Jesus Christ, dwells in bodily form. The body cannot be viewed as evil for God took up residence in the body. The Gnostics, whose beliefs later became a serious threat to the Early Church, believed in the separation of the soul and body. They believed that spirit was good and matter was evil. They held to the view that Christ took up the body of the human Jesus at baptism and left his body at the cross. Christ only used the human body for his mission on earth. He did not need the body any longer once the mission was over. This teaching was heretical and strongly opposed by Church Fathers like Irenaeus who wrote against the movement.

---

5. Cited by Willard, *The Spirit of Disciplines*. 81–82.
6. Benner, *Soulful Spirituality*, 79.
7. Cox, "The Physical Body in Spiritual Formation" 281.

Scripture is clear that Jesus was birthed by Mary. He was conceived by the Holy Spirit in Mary's womb. He spent the normal number of months in his mother's womb during the gestation period. He took on human flesh and never left his body. He grew up catering to the needs of the body like all of us. He needed to eat, sleep, wash, wear clothes, and trained as a carpenter using his hands. Like all physical bodies, Jesus' body took time to grow. The apostle Luke wrote in his Gospel that Jesus grew in wisdom and stature, and in favor with God and men (Luke 2:52).

## The Body is a Vehicle for Divine Work

The body, as a temple of the Holy Spirit, is holy and used as a vehicle or instrument by God to do his divine work in our lives. Our role is to offer parts of our bodies by submitting to God's will and pleasure. Since our bodies are predisposed to sin due to our fallen nature, we need to train our bodies well in order for God to do his marvelous work in us. Willard points out that if a body is trained well using tools and raw materials, its power extends beyond the little power resident in it. For example, a skilled person with a bat can hit a ball faster and higher than just using the hand to throw it. A person skilled in playing a piano can make great music than without one. Similarly, a person who has trained well in applying the spiritual disciplines of prayer, worship, meditation, solitude, fellowship, and so on, will be able to mesh his limited power with a greater power beyond his body. All these spiritual practices are bodily in nature.[8] When our bodies are well-trained in the spiritual disciplines we "allow our spirit ever-increasing sway over our embodied selves. They help by assisting the ways of God's Kingdom to take the place of the habits of sin embedded in our bodies."[9]

The whole body, trained by the disciplines and under the rule of the Spirit, is made available and offered to God as an instrument of righteousness. Saint Antony spoke of this:

---

8. Porter, *The Willardian Corpus*, 253–54.
9. Willard, *The Spirit of the Disciplines*, 86.

# AN EMBODIED SPIRITUALITY

> The Spirit, combining with the mind . . . Teaches it to keep the body in order—all of it, from head to foot: the eyes to see with purity; the ears, to listen in peace, not to delight in slander, gossip and abuse; the tongue, to say only what is good . . . the hands, to be raised in prayer and for works of mercy. . . ; the stomach, to keep the use of food and drink within the necessary limits. . . ; the feet, to walk rightly and follow the will of God . . . In this way the whole body becomes trained in good and undergoes a change, submitting to the rule of the Holy Spirit, so that in the end it begins in some measure to share in such properties of the spiritual body, as it is to receive at the resurrection of the just.[10]

## Paying Close Attention to the Body

Paul wants us to know that our bodies are not our own. They are bought with a price and therefore we need to glorify God with our bodies (1 Cor 6:19–20). How can we glorify God with our bodies? Besides taking good care of our bodies, we also need to pay close attention to our bodies as well. Tilden Edwards, director of the Shalem Institute of Spiritual Formation, notes that attention to the body is integral to the spiritual life.[11] Sometimes our minds can deceive us but not our bodies. When I am waiting to go on to the stage to preach, my mind tells me that everything are under control, but my body tells a different story. A sweaty palm, tapping of fingers or legs, and the shifting of my body are telling signs that I am nervous. I will take a few deep breaths to calm my nerves and to tell my mind not to panic. The body has an intuitive way of knowing before the mind does. Belden Lane, an avid hiker himself, says that he relies on his bodily cues while walking in the wilderness. He says,

> The body is an extremely reliable guide. It knows instinctively how to move over difficult terrain, when to stop for rest, how to breathe deeply and relax in crisis

---

10. Cited by Edwards, *Living in the Presence*, 16–17.
11. Ibid., 17.

situations . . . What the mind hardly fathoms, the body already knows.[12]

The mind can follow the lead of the body. We need to still our bodies first in order to still our minds. Conversely, our bodies cannot stay still if our minds are filled with many things that we must do. One way to clear our thoughts is to take a walk. Walking relaxes our muscles which also frees our minds from those anxious thoughts. Sometimes our bodies can assess reality more than the brain. For example, my body is telling me that I am getting defensive when I fold my arms tightly while talking. I need to prompt myself mentally not to succumb to a defensive mode. I immediately unfold my arms. This gesture of unfolding my arms tells the mind not to be intimidated by the ongoing conversation. Interestingly, Tilden Edwards points out that what we do with our hands in prayer can influence our minds as well. If we fold our hands, it tempts our minds to shy away from participation. Hands tightly interlocked will make our minds tense. If we pray with raised arms, our minds too are raised to God. If our hands are loosely open, our minds will open a space for God.[13]

Listening to our bodies can impact our walk with God. Elouise Renich Fraser in *Confessions of a Beginning Theologian* has this to say:

> My body, once ignored and despised, has become an ally in the reorientation of my internal and external life. It lets me know when I'm running away, avoiding yet another God's invitations to look into my past and the way it binds me as a theologian. I can't trust my mind as often as I trust my body. My mind tries to talk me into business as usual, but my body isn't fooled. Insomnia, intestinal pain and diarrhea let me know there's work to be done.[14]

---

12. Lane, *Backpacking with the Saints*, 7.
13. Edwards, *Living in the Presence*, 27.
14. Fraser, *Confessions of a Beginning Theologian*, 31.

# AN EMBODIED SPIRITUALITY

## The Daily Examen

What we feel in our bodies may not necessary be taken up by our minds. We tend not to trust emotions because they are subjective. We prefer to think rationally and so we trust our judgment using our brains more than our feelings. Not to take a serious view of our emotions is to be alienated from our bodies. Our emotions are manifestations of our bodies just as the senses are connected with our minds. Whether we are sad, happy, disappointed or excited, these emotions will show in our bodies. I pull a long face and even shed some tears when I am sad. I jump with joy when I am happy or excited. When I am disappointed, I hang down my head.

Ignatius of Loyola developed a spiritual discipline called the Daily Examen of consciousness to detect the subtle movements of God in our lives. This discipline helps us to have a greater awareness of God's presence in our lives. It requires us to be in touch with our emotions during the course of the day. These emotions can be positive or negative feelings. He named the positive emotions, consolations and the negative emotions, desolations. Consolations are moments when we experience stillness and peace. Desolations are when we experience fear and anxiety. During the course of the day, we encounter numerous events, people or things. How we respond to these will determine whether these are consolations or desolations. If we are disturbed, fearful or anxious by something we hear, a person we meet or an event we encounter, these manifested emotions will turn us away from God. God may be speaking to us, using these desolations, about our need to repent, to reconcile and forgive, or to change our ways or conduct to others. Conversely, we may feel joyful over an event that is uplifting or having inner peace due to a wise action taken. Consolations are used by God to turn our desires to him. We are able to discern God's hand leading and guiding us in these moments. Getting in touch with our positive and negative emotions and reviewing them at the end of the day will help us to discern the hand of God at work in our lives. This spiritual practice helps us to know ourselves and God better.

## Taking Care of the Body

We need to take good care of our bodies apart from paying attention to how our bodies feel. We take good care of the body not because it is central to our life but we want to use it for God. To many people in the world, the body is the main driver of life. The world worships the body and takes great pains to care for it. Having a great and beautiful body will be the envy of others. The body is used for self-gratification and indulgence. No wonder most of our time is devoted in taking care of our bodies. Our worries are centered around the need to care for our bodies: what to eat, drink or wear. Jesus tells us that we should not worry over these things that our bodies need. Instead, we should use our bodies to serve God and his Kingdom (Matt 6:25).

Good exercise and diet are essential to a healthy body. I just came back from a hiking trip with some friends this morning. The trip took almost three hours to hike up to the highest point in the Penang National Park. The hike was good even though we had to climb some steep inclines and walked through dense foliage in some parts of the forest. The ferns were so thick in some places that we literally had to wade our way through. We came back exhausted, sweaty, and with bruises and cuts on our legs. I have a good power nap in the afternoon to rejuvenate and to give my body a well-deserved rest. I will feel the aching muscles in my legs and body the following day. I climb regularly. I used to jog when I was younger, but climbing is preferred now because it causes less injury. I also have regular workouts at home. I do push-ups, planking, and weights during my workout. These are good exercises for those whose bodies are no longer young.

We must also learn to stuff our bodies with healthy foods. We are what we eat. I prefer raw vegetables like salads than cooked vegetables fried in oil. Fast and fried foods are definitely not good for the body. A low carbohydrate diet with less sugar and salt is a plus for the body. I prefer a light breakfast in the morning: yogurt and oats with coffee served later. As a Penangnite living in a place where people love to eat, I am used to eating all kinds of food.

Lately, I avoid eating out too often. I do not want to indulge myself by eating foods that are not good for the body. Outside foods cater to the taste buds than to the health of the body. Our bodies are more alert and alive to God when we exercise and eat well.

## The Importance of Sleep

Another area we should look into is sleep if we want to take good care of our bodies. We are so used to sleep that we do not think much about it. If we use one third of our life sleeping, it must be important to us. The psalmist has something to teach us on why sleep is important:

> Unless the Lord builds the house, its builders labor in vain. Unless the Lord watches over the city, the watchmen stand guard in vain. In vain you rise early and stay up late, toiling for food to eat—for he grants sleep to those he loves (Ps 127:1–2).

We carry our worries to bed. No wonder we cannot sleep well in the night. We toss and turn thinking about the house we are building or whether we are safe when sleeping. Recently thieves broke into my house and I lost some money and valuables. Since then, I am more conscious about safeguarding my environment. I check all the locks in my house before I go to bed. Sometimes I am alerted to some unusual sounds and I may want to get up from my bed just to make sure. I also know of people who literally lost weight when their house underwent a renovation. They worried over whether the job could complete on time. They were frustrated with dishonest contractors who never delivered what was promised. They were afraid of cost overruns, shoddy workmanship, and inferior materials used.

The psalmist reminds us that in sleep we are yielding our control to God. When we sleep we are trusting God to take over our worries. This clearly shows that we are not God since God does not sleep. We need to know our limitations as mortals since we are not in control over at least one third of our life. Sleep shows our dependence on our Creator. Philip Yancey, best selling evangelical author, in one of his sermons portrayed sleep as God sending us to bed as patients with a sickness. He described this sickness as "a chronic tendency to think that we are in control and that our work is indispensable."[15]

We know that the more we want to sleep, the more sleep escapes us. No matter how hard we try to sleep, we remain wide awake. Sleep is a gift given to us by God. In this manner, sleep can serve as an analogy of spiritual growth.[16] We cannot solely depend on spiritual disciplines to grow spiritually. Spiritual disciplines can only provide the condition or instrument for growth. Growth cannot be earned or based on our own efforts. Like sleep, it is a gift of grace from God. We need to regard sleep as a spiritual discipline if we take sleep seriously. We have to have enough sleep to rest our bodies and to pay heed to the body's rhythms. It is not helpful to subject our bodies to late nights in order to catch up with our assignments or work. Sleep is used to balance our compulsive work habits.[17]

So is Sabbath keeping. Work is the place where we can easily succumb to idolatry because it is where we can exercise control and feel most competent. Work can become our idol if we are not careful. We know of workaholics who put their work above all else. Many work overtime. Some even bring their sleeping bags to their office in case they need to sleep over due to urgent deadlines. This happen to aspiring young people who work in high-tech companies. Sabbath, like sleep, frees us from taking charge and to let God have control. He will keep the world moving even if we take a day off from work. To Eugene Peterson, Sabbath keeping is our weekly housecleaning. It is to begin the week uncluttered with idols. It is to detach ourselves from the world's way of doing things which usually compels us to take things into our own hands.[18]

---

15. Yancey, taken from www.hopeingod.org/document/brief-theology-sleep.

16. McMartin, "Sleep, Sloth, and Sanctification" 261.

17. Peterson, *A Long Obedience in the Same Direction*, 103.

18. Peterson, *Christ Plays in Ten Thousand Places*, 128–29.

# AN EMBODIED SPIRITUALITY

## Not to Abuse or Misuse the Body

Taking care of the body also means that we cannot subject our bodies to misuse or abuse. Sexual immorality and gluttony use the body as a source of sensual gratification. To indulge in these activities or habits are to use the body not to honor God but for self-indulgence. Many of us do not normally view gluttony as sinful. Gluttony, besides lust, was included as one of the seven deadly sins by the early Christians. Paul calls on us not to make an idol of our stomachs besides warning about sexual immorality. Addictions, like drugs and alcohol, are harming our bodies. They will affect or disrupt our ability to function normally. Life can be tough and addictions are to numb us from the painful realities of life. Addicted people prefer to live in a world of illusions. They are not willing to face the pain and brokenness which life mercilessly offers us from time to time. Christians who view their bodies as God's temple should stay away from these habits. Our bodies are holy, set apart for God. Piercing our skin with tattoos may appear to be cool and trendy but this is also a form of bodily abuse which the Bible does not condone (Lev 19:28). The disfiguring of the body was a pagan practice at the time of Moses. It is still true today.

We better take our bodies seriously if they are vehicles for God to do his divine work in us. Paying close attention to our bodies will help to impact our walk with Jesus. We must not suppress or neglect our bodies. Instead we should take good care of them for God's sake. We look at physical exercises, good diet, and sleep as part and parcel of living a disciplined spiritual life. It is pointless for us to fast until we develop gastric problems or endure sleepless nights in prayer vigils until we cannot function properly the next day. These acts of sacrifices may look good outwardly but they can do more harm than good to our spiritual lives if we do not value our bodies which are made by God. Some neglect their bodies thinking that they are impediments to the soul's journey with God.

The physical body is rooted in physical time and space. We cannot transport ourselves back to the past or forward to the future. Part of our spirituality is to attune ourselves to the present moment. We find it difficult to be present to the moment because we are easily bothered by past events or anxious about what will happen in the future. These occupations and preoccupations are impediments to the soul's journey with God. We should learn to value such moments for they are profitable to our souls. We become more alive to God and the things around us when we present ourselves with an undivided mind to the present moment.

## Questions for Reflection and Discussion

1. Do you take your body seriously in spiritual matters? Why?
2. How can your body help you in your spiritual growth?
3. Do you pay close attention to your body? How can you detect what God is telling you through your body?
4. Have you been taking good care of your body? Has your body been neglected or suppressed? What steps are you taking to address this problem?

*Chapter 4*

# THE PRESENT MOMENT

> Moments are holy doorways where we are lifted out of time and we encounter the sacred in the most ordinary of acts.
>
> —CHRISTINE VALTERS PAINTNER[1]

## The Three Questions

AN EMPEROR WAS LOOKING for answers to three important questions. A reward would be given to the one who could answer these questions correctly. No one in his kingdom could answer these three questions to his satisfaction. Finally, he decided to visit a wise man who lived up on the mountain. He left his guards at the foot of the mountain while he made his way to the hermit's house. He disguised himself as a farmer so that the hermit could not recognize him. When he arrived he saw the holy man digging his garden. The emperor approached him and said, "I am here to ask for your help to answer three questions: When is the best time to do each thing? Who are the most important person to work with? What is the most important thing to do at each time? The old man listened but went on digging and said nothing in reply. The emperor offered to help him dig since he looked exhausted.

---

1. Paintner, "Cultivating the Eyes of the Heart" 28.

The old man gladly handed the hoe to him. The emperor again asked the hermit the three questions after working for some time. The hermit again did not answer. The emperor, at this time, was wondering whether he had wasted his trip visiting the old man.

Suddenly, he saw a man coming out from the forest. He was wounded and fell unconscious at his feet. The emperor helped the injured man by attending to his wound. The man was taken to the house after the wound was cleaned and dressed. The next day the man woke up and saw the emperor. He told the emperor, in a weak voice, that he was his sworn enemy. He actually planned to ambush and kill him. He plotted to ambush him when he heard that the emperor was seeing the hermit. He came across the emperor's attendants and was wounded by them before he could reach the emperor. He was lucky to escape and ran to take refuge in the hermit's house. He then asked for the emperor's forgiveness which the emperor was happy to oblige. The emperor instructed his attendants to accompany the man to his home and take good care of him. He then turned to the hermit and asked the same three questions. The hermit told the emperor that his questions were already answered. The emperor was puzzled and asked for clarification.

The wise man said that the emperor stayed back to help him instead of going home. If he had gone home earlier he would meet his enemy along the way and be killed. So the time he used to dig the garden was the best time. The most important person was of course the hermit himself and the most important thing to do was to help the hermit dig the garden. As for the wounded man, the best time was when he helped dress the wound of his enemy. If he did not show compassion and helped the wounded man, he would die from his wounds and he would lose the chance to be reconciled with his enemy. The most important person was the person he helped, and the most important thing to do was to take care of his wounds. The old hermit gave this advice to the king:

> Remember that there is only one important time and that is now. The present moment is the only time over which we have dominion. The most important person is always the person you are with, who is right before you,

*THE PRESENT MOMENT*

for who knows if you will have dealings with any other person in the future? The most important pursuit is making the person standing at your side happy, for that alone is the pursuit of life.²

## Present to the Moment

I moved house more than a dozen times since I began serving God many years ago. Each move was a transition for us. During this time, our minds and hearts were no longer present with our current place and people. We began to think of our next move and about the new people we would meet and new place we would stay. I remember the time when we decided to move from Penang to Nanning, a city in Southern China. The name "Nanning" in Chinese means "southern peace". I had not heard of the city before and I was curious because the name struck a chord in me. So I spent considerable amount of time googling to find out more about the city. My heart was no longer with the present place and people that I worked with. Though bodily I was still there but mentally I had transported myself into the future. It is easy for us to lose touch with the now. As the hermit wisely observes, the most important time is the present moment. The past is over and the future is yet to come. What we have is the present. Our existence is rooted in the present and what we do now reflects who we are, and not what we ought or should be.

"Transitions," as Roger Owens cautions us, "is a ripe time to recognize the work of God in our lives. It is also one of the easiest times to miss the work of God, distracted as we might be by fantasies about what's up the road . . ."³

De Caussade was an 18th century ordained priest who lived in Toulouse in Southern France. His most celebrated work, *The Sacrament of the Present Moment*, is still in print today. In his conferences on the spiritual life with the nuns, he shared that God spoke to the

2. Story adapted from Thich Nhat Hanh's *The Miracle of Mindfulness*, 69–75.

3. Owens, "Keep In Touch" 18.

individual through what happened moment by moment. Her duty was to be able to discern such moments with the goal to obey him immediately. He went on to say that "the only condition necessary for this state of self-surrender is the present moment in which the soul, light as a feather, fluid as water, innocent as a child, responds to every movement of grace like a floating balloon."[4]

God promised Moses that his Presence would go with the nation Israel. Moses asked to see God's face but God said that no one who saw his face could live. He told Moses that he would pass by him when he hid himself in a cleft of a rock. God would use his hand to cover his glory and would remove it when he passed by Moses. Moses would see his back and not his face (Exod 33:21–23). Often God passes by us everyday without us knowing his presence. "Moment by moment," writes Benner, "Presence comes to us, and all that we have to do to encounter it is be present ourselves. Being present is a brush with the Holy One."[5] God, in whom we move and have our being, passes by us everyday but are we present to those sacred moments? If the present moment is so important to our spiritual lives, why do we fail to embrace it? Why is it difficult to be present ourselves? What are the hindrances that we face that detach us from the present moment?

## The Hurried Life

The hurried life is one reason why we have difficulty presenting ourselves. Time is no longer a gift from God for us to enjoy. It has become a commodity for us to use optimally. We run from one activity to another for we thrive better on doing than being. We feel bored or guilty if we have ample time on our hands. So we keep ourselves busy and this running about gives us a good feeling of accomplishment. We hardly have the time or see the need to slow down in order to embrace the present moment that passes by us.

Thich Nhat Hanh, a well known Zen master, has this advice for us: when we eat, we eat; when we wash the dishes, we wash

---

4. De Caussade, *The Sacrament of the Present Moment*, xiii–xiv.

5. Benner, *Presence and Encounter*, 25.

## THE PRESENT MOMENT

dishes. When we eat, our bodies may be present but our thoughts are far away. We may not even recall exactly what we have eaten! When we wash dishes we want to finish doing the task as soon as we can so that we can get on to the next task. In this way we are no longer attentive to what we are doing in the present moment. We fail to live because we fail to live the actual moment. We are detached from the present because we are attached to the future. Thich Nhat Hanh suggests that when we drink tea, we need to drink it slowly and reverently "as if it is the axis which the whole earth revolves - slowly, evenly, without rushing toward the future.[6]

### Ways of Slowing Down

I know that it is difficult to slow down. In a digitized society where modern gadgets are used to get things done as quickly and conveniently as possible, slowing down requires a conscious and intended effort on our part. One way is to practice walking slowly. I realize that this is not easy for those who own cars. Even for a short distance, we prefer to drive than walk. If we are in a hurry to reach our destination we will not slow down even when we walk. We should take the slow walk as a destination instead. We are alerted to whatever that may come to us through our senses as we walk. We should not try to think and judge too much but use our senses to absorb the things that are happening around us through listening, touching, smelling, seeing, and tasting.

We are made aware of our bodily movements as we walk slowly. We are conscious of the pull of gravity that sinks our feet to the ground. We begin to take note of our breathing. We may try walking barefooted. Walking barefooted is a good way to feel the earth's texture underneath out feet. The Native Americans prefer to walk barefooted because to them the earth is the source of sacred energy. This may also be the reason why they prefer sitting on the ground when they have their council meetings. As we walk slowly and taking in the sights and sounds around us, we become, for the

---

6. Hanh, *The Miracle of Mindfulness*, 4–5, 30.

first time, more conscious to the things in the environment that escape us when we are in a hurry to go somewhere.

We begin the day by waking up. Our minds are up and running within seconds after we wake up. We are thinking of things to do. We begin by making our bed, drawing the curtains, brushing our teeth, washing up, cooking breakfast, getting dressed, and getting ready for work. We can spend some quiet moments in bed instead of getting up immediately and attend to a list of things to do. We can practice waking up slowly. Take some moments to be aware of the presence of our bodies by taking notice of our breathing, the presence of God who breathes his life into us, and the presence of the furniture in the room.[7] This will help us face the day with calmness and confidence. We need to begin the day slowly in order to slow down.

God has enacted the Sabbath to help us slow down. Sabbath is a time for us to stop working and to pause, rest, and reflect in the midst of busyness. In the same vein, winter is nature's way of resting and rejuvenating. Winter is the time for animals to hibernate, for leafless tress to conserve in order to prepare for spring, and for humans to stay indoors to avoid the cold. I remember walking on the snow in winter. We cannot walk fast even with snow boots. We need to slow down. Walking on the snow requires us to pay attention to our every step in case we slip and fall. This allows us to notice things along the way; things we hardly notice in other seasons. Unlike spring, summer, and autumn, winter is the season when things are slowing down. We begin to see and feel things with a renewed perspective in the stillness and simplicity of winter.[8] It is not surprising that brother Lawrence, a Carmelite lay brother who wrote the classic *The Practice of the Presence of God*, was first drawn to God by the sight of a leafless tree in winter. In the stillness of winter, I can literally feel my heart beating restfully under my chest when I wake up from sleep; I can hear the distant drone of a solitary plane that fly past at the exact time each day;

---

7. Bloom, *Beginning to Pray*, 85.
8. Rensberger, "The Holiness of Winter" 35–39.

and I am more aware of the fast changing light due to the short days and long nights.

## The Thought Life

Some people are good at multitasking. They can do several things at any one time. They switch from one activity to another. But they are not focused or aware of the activity at hand. While doing one thing, their minds are thinking of the next task. To be attentive we can only do one thing at a time. I cannot keep on writing this chapter if someone comes to me and start a conversation. I need to stop writing and begin to pay attention to the other person. Only when he walks away can I continue writing. Our thoughts can detach us from being present to the moment. The poet Dan Gerber was taking a short walk from his home. Not long after he left his house, he realized that he had been taking his house with him. He remembered, while walking, that he had unfinished tasks that were waiting for him to do: unanswered letters and telephone calls, and windows that needed caulking. He had left his mind at home. He lamented that his feet had been taking a walk without him.[9]

The two disciples on the road to Emmaus were preoccupied with the recent events that happened in Jerusalem. They did not recognize Jesus as the risen Lord even though he was walking with them on the road. Their bodies were with Jesus but their thoughts and feelings were far away. They allowed their thoughts and feelings over the tragic event to blur their vision. They hardly noticed that God was passing by them. If they had not retained Jesus to stay for the evening meal their eyes would not be opened and recognized their beloved Lord through the breaking of bread.

How can we prevent the thoughts and feelings from invading our consciousness? We cannot stop them but we can recognize and acknowledge their presence just like a security guard who scans the faces of people passing through a security checkpoint. We should not fight against these distractions or irritated by them.

9. Gerber, "Walking in Tierra del Fuego" 66–67. Cited by Lane, *Backpacking*, 106.

If we do, we will immediately lose being present to the moment. By naming them we are able to allow our thoughts and feelings to pass through our minds as they float down our stream of consciousness. We don't resist them or retain them. We need to learn to detach ourselves from those thoughts and feelings that are dragging us away from what is happening in the present moment. It is when we are in deep conversation with a friend we have not seen for a long while and someone we know comes along. We nod to acknowledge her presence and continue with our conversation. Someone says that we cannot keep the birds from flying over our heads but we can stop them from building a nest on our heads.

## The Lectio Divina of Ordinary Things

Instead of seeing the present moment as it truly is, we have the tendency to bring to it our interpretations and expectations. In other words, we define reality before we experience it.[10] There are two ways for us to read Scripture. We can interpret Scripture by extracting information revealed by the text. In knowing the historical, cultural, and literary context of the text, we are given enough information to interpret the text with confidence. We come to the text expecting to glean information that we know is there. We only need to use the right tools and principles of interpretation to explore the text. The other way of reading is the *lectio divina* or spiritual reading. We approach the text slowly with an open mind, waiting and listening for a word or phrase that shimmers or resonates with us. The word or phrase is God's voice speaking to us in the present moment. We are not looking for any particular piece of information that can help us to master the text. We simply allow the unexpected word or phrase to come to us on its own accord.

We can use the practice of *lectio divina* to include the ordinary things of life. We allow God to speak to us in the most unexpected manner when we present ourselves to the moment. Many of us have difficulty finding God in the mundane affairs of living. We think that God can only be encountered in a preached sermon,

---

10. Lane, *Backpacking with the Saints*, 98.

## THE PRESENT MOMENT

in reading a text of Scripture, in the worship service, in the church, and on Sundays. Unconsciously, we have confined God to only one day a week. The rest of the days he is not on our radar screen because we do not expect him to be there. The two disciples on the way to Emmaus faced a similar problem. They did not expect the risen Lord to pass by them. God is everywhere and he is not restricted to a place or time. Sue Monk Kidd, best known for her novel *The Secret Life of Bees*, writes that if we want to be present in those moments with him, we need to be open ourselves by putting out a welcome mat.[11] We can also shake a roll of baking foil and let out its flaming shine and shimmering sound. The Jesuit poet Gerard Manley Hopkins declares that "the world is charged with the grandeur of God. It will flame out, like shining from shook foil." We can present ourselves to those shimmering moments when we "brush with the Holy One" instead of looking for information and expecting God to meet us at our appointed time and place.

Journalist and writer Philip Tonybee had a brush with God one day when he went walking in the Forest of Dean. He was struggling with depression at the time. Like brother Lawrence, a single tree he came across in his walk opened his eyes to a changed world. He wrote these entries in his journal:

> Pouring with rain yesterday made gardening impossible; so I put on my ferocious boots and set out for a serious walk. The first for months. The boots splendidly increased my sense of purpose; not of destination, but of walking for walking's sake. A free and purposeful man! And a changed world! For on this walk I stopped several times and looked at a single tree as I haven't done for years. No, as I've never done in my life before. The tree was there and now, in its own immediate and peculiar right: that tree and no other. And I was acutely here-and-now as I stared at it, unhampered by past or future. Intense happiness.

A week later he made another entry in his journal about the tree:

11. Kidd, *God's Joyful Surprise*, 132–33.

> Tree scrutiny... I stand apart and look; looking I respect, almost to the point of love. But what I hope to be loving is God; not because he "made" the tree but because he gave me the power to see it with such intensity and clarity.[12]

## The Impediments Associated with the Present Moment

What are the impediments that prevent us from being present to the moment? Busyness is a hindrance, so we need to slow down in order to notice the shimmering presence of God around us. We also need to be aware of the thoughts and feelings that distance us from embracing the present moment. We cannot resist these intruding thoughts but we can release and not retain them. We need to accept the present moment as it truly is and not to bring with it our interpretations and expectations. In other words, we are not seeking information to satisfy our minds but to seek his presence by opening ourselves to him. We cannot be present to the moment if our minds are too full. A mind filled with ideas and opinions is also a divided mind. We cannot stay focus if our minds are divided. What are the ways we can be present to the moment?

### The Impediment of Busyness

Busyness can stop us from being present to the moment. One way to overcome this is to stop and do nothing for a period of time. It can be a couple of minutes or longer. This stopping time is to help us to be completely in the present. We should not allow anything, be it phone call or a knock on the door, to disturb us from the present moment. Anthony Bloom, bishop of the Russian Orthodox Church in Great Britain and Ireland, has this advice for us in his book, *Beginning To Pray*:

> You sit down and say, "I am seated, I am doing nothing, I will do nothing for five minutes, and then relax,

---

12. Tonybee, *Part of a Journey: An Autobiographical Journal - 1977–79*, 56–59.

and continually throughout this time realize, "I am here in the presence of God, in my own presence and in the presence of all the furniture around me, just still and moving nowhere."[13]

This exercise if done regularly will help us to slow down. We can increase the time gradually in order to make it a regular pattern of our life. The monks in the monasteries have their schedule prayer times which they call the Daily Office. These are scheduled times when they will stop whatever they are doing and be present with God. The morning and evening praise are the basic hours of the Daily Office. Some monastic communities observe one or more of the other five hours as well. They are prime, terce, sext, none, and matins. This Daily Office was practiced as early as the 6th century AD. The Rule of Saint Benedict writes: "On hearing the signal for an hour of the divine office, the monk will immediately set aside what he has in hand and go with utmost speed . . . Indeed, nothing is to be preferred to the Work of God (that is, the Daily Office)."

## The Impediment of Thoughts and Feelings

Our thoughts and feelings can distance us from being present to the moment. There is a story of a young monk who was told by his elder to stay in his cell and pray. The young novice came back the next day announcing to the elder monk that the door to the cell was old and needed replacing. The old man again told him to sit in his cell and pray. He came back the following day with another complaint. He noticed that the roof of his cell was getting old and needed replacing. The older monk finally told him that what was really needed replacing was his wandering thoughts.[14]

Our minds can be too full to be truly present. We are living in a wordy world. Everywhere we go we are constantly bombarded with words that call on us to "eat me, use me, take me, and love me." Modern technologies make possible the free flow of information

---

13. Bloom, *Beginning to Pray*, 85–86.
14. Lane, *Backpacking*, 106.

at our finger tips. We can freely dispense our opinions, ideas, and comments using apps like *Facebook* or *Twitter* on our mobile phones. Their ease of use can create problems for the users. They may regret making certain remarks too quickly without thinking of the consequences. Snail mail is different because it needs some time to send whereas email or text messages can be sent instantly at a click of a mouse or a touch of an icon. The time taken to send by snail mail will allow them some space to digest and reflect over the use or misuse of words.

A Zen story goes like this. Once, a university professor visited a Zen master to ask about Zen. The professor seemed to be an intelligent person with a good grasp of common knowledge. He also liked to dominate the discussion with his thoughts and ideas. The master served him tea by pouring it into his cup. He poured until the visitor's cup was overflowing with tea. The professor noticed the cup and said, "The cup is full and no more can go in!" The master looked at him and replied, "I know. You are full of opinions and speculations like this cup. How can I teach you Zen unless you first empty your cup?"[15]

## The Impediment of Judgment

We need to suspend judgment in order to be present to the moment. In other words, we must learn to accept the moment as it is and not thinking whether we are pleased with it or not. This shows that we are not content or happy with what happens at the moment if we resist the present moment. The present moment is most important to us at the time and we should welcome it with an open mind whatever it may be. When we make a judgment, our focus has shifted from the present moment to our thoughts. We are no longer available to the present moment.

Anthony Bloom shared that when he first became a physician, his mind was on those waiting patiently in the waiting room. He was so anxious to clear the queue in the waiting room that he was not present to the patient he was treating. He wanted to clear each

---

15. Reps, *Zen Flesh, Zen Bones*, 5.

# THE PRESENT MOMENT

patient in his clinic as quickly as possible to shorten the queue. His lack of focus led him to ask the questions more than once and do the same examinations two or three times. When he had finished treating the patient he could not recollect the things he had just done. He felt uneasy about the whole matter and so decided that he would see his patient as if he or she was the only person in the clinic. He would used a few minutes to engage the patient in small talk the moment he felt that he was pushed to hurry. He realized that when he was completely present to the immediate task at hand, he spent half the time doing it and was able to recollect all the things that he had done before.[16]

Our minds are divided when we pass judgment and have strong opinions. Sue Monk Kidd points out that it is not easy to be fully present to the other person when we often received people with a divided mind. She writes:

> To be fully present is not to pass judgment on the other person, wanting to convert her to our point of view, desiring her appreciation, wondering what others may think, worrying about the weather, or generally getting caught up in one's own feelings, desires, and opinions of the moment.[17]

It is difficult to be truly present when our minds are constantly bombarded with sounds, images, and words that come from all directions. We cannot escape from these distractions while living in an information age. Information is cheaply and easily available using our mobile phones. The first thing we want to do when we wake up is to have access to the information at hand. This has become a habit for many people. Losing the hand phone is like losing an arm or leg. They momentarily become immobilized and disorientated. This can be a traumatic experience for some people who are addicted to social media. This is complicated by our hurried lifestyle where we hardly find the time to dissect the information we are

16. Bloom, *Beginning to Pray*, 88.
17. Kidd, "Live Welcoming to All," 9.

getting. We are not able, in most cases, to prevent these thoughts and feelings prompted by the information we receive to invade our consciousness. We lack focus and become distracted. We are easily swayed and become judgmental by bringing our interpretations and expectations to the situation. All these will not help us to present ourselves or to stay focus on the present moment.

One way to deal with these distractions is to slow down. Slowing down is not easy for we are used to a hurried life running from one activity to another. It requires deliberate and intentional effort on us. We can take time to be aware and be conscious of the moment. We can cease doing anything and just take time to notice the things that are happening around us. We can savor and enjoy the mysteries of life around us without always seeking for information or answers. An open and attentive heart is needed to see things with a new perspective. We are surrounded by wonders everywhere and it is up to us to notice them. The ordinary things in the world are percolated by the divine. We can see the world with a sense of wonder and expecting to be surprised by it.

## Questions for Reflection and Discussion

1. Are you more concern about the future and not the present moment? Why?
2. What are the preoccupations and occupations in your mind right now that prevent you to be present to the moment?
3. What are the impediments that prevent you from being present to the moment? How can you hope to overcome them?
4. Why is it important to your spiritual life that you adopt the habit of being present to the moment?

*Chapter 5*

# THE GIFT OF WONDER

Wonder is the wellspring of love . . . and love, in the end, is what drives us to a passion for all things wild and at risk.

—ABRAHAM HESCHEL[1]

## The Capacity to Wonder

ONE FINE DAY A farmer took his son to visit the Grand Canyon. The immense size of the canyon could be overwhelming for a young kid. The canyon was a mile deep in some places. The child, standing at the edge of the Grand Canyon for the first time, was astonished and amazed at the sight. He had never seen anything like this before. With mouth opened in awe and eyes filled with wonder he couldn't resist himself. He threw his hands to the air, jumping and exclaimed widely, "Wow! Look, look!" The farmer, resting his chin in his hand, said, "Yeah, what a place to lose a cow!"

Children tend to view things differently from adults. When I was a child I always looked forward to an outing with excitement. One fine day my dad's friend drove us to the botanical gardens. He managed to borrow a car for the trip. In those days not many people owned cars. It was a memorable trip though I have forgotten all the things I saw along the way. The only thing I remember

---

1. Dresner, ed. *I Asked for Wonder,* 2–3.

vividly were the monkeys loitering along the road that led to the gardens. We stopped by the roadside and fed a bunch of monkeys with peanuts. That was probably the first time I sat in a car. Everything was new and fresh to a young mind. I began to discover a new world outside my home. I also remember a time when my dad put me on the back seat of his bicycle and together we rode to see a movie. That was probably the first time that I entered a theater. I never knew that the theater was such a dark place! We were momentarily blinded until someone showed us to our seats with a torchlight. I took numerous trips to the gardens and the movie house when I grew up but the excitement was not there anymore.

It is interesting to know that children under the age of six have one of the highest survival rates of those who are lost in the wilderness. Small children who are lost in a wild place tend not to wander around too much. They are intrigued by the things around them due to the innate ability to wonder and are more inclined to stop and rest when needed. They may even find a suitable spot to sleep if they feel tired. Adults react differently when lost. Adults tend to panic when they realize that they are lost. They move fast and usually heading in the wrong direction! They will feel exhausted and disoriented after some time of frantic running.[2]

As we grow older, taller, and wiser, we lack the capacity to wonder. We no longer see the world with awe like a child. It is no longer a world filled with mystery. It is a disenchanted world dominated by science and technology. Science seeks answers from nature and technology uses these answers to master nature for our advancement and progress. Rational thinking diminishes our capacity to wonder. The gift of wonder calls us back to view the world as mysterious and sacred. There are two ways to respond to the world around us: the way of reason and the way of wonder.[3] Reason seeks to tame, exploit, and to gain control over the world. Wonder, on the other hand, does not seek for information or answers. It responds to the mysteries of life with an open and attentive heart. It does not impose judgment but receives the world as it is.

2. Gonzales, *Deep Survival*, 170–71.
3. Heschel, *Man is Not Alone*, 13.

# THE GIFT OF WONDER

A child spends most of her time at play. She does not feel bored easily while living in a world filled with wonder. She is intrigued by the things around her world. She can spend hours indulging in imaginative play with her favorite doll or game. An adult spends most of his time working. This is where, using his knowledge and skills, he can gain mastery and competence over his environment. Information and competence, which are highly valued by those who work, squeeze out wonder in the workplace.[4] The workplace cannot tolerate wastage in terms of time and resources. The worker has no time to pause and reflect over his work. He does not want any surprises at the work place. He wants a controlled and predictable environment to do his work. His identity is formed by the working conditions that are intolerant of the mysteries of life. It is not surprising that as he grows older he no longer sees the world with the eyes of a child. He has lost the capacity to wonder.

## The Need to Nurture Wonder

Why is it necessary for us to develop and nurture this sense of wonder? The human spirit needs it. The human spirit will not be on a quest to explore the unknown without wonder and the underlying curiosity. When humans looked at the dark sky filled with lights from afar they wondered about what these stars were like. For centuries they had no clue what they were like until they invented a telescope to help them see clearer and further. They were intrigued by what they saw. So they built bigger and more powerful instruments to scan the skies.

In 1990, the Hubble Space Telescope launched high above the earth's atmosphere in outer space was able to capture images of our universe and the millions of stars in other galaxies. Scientists using the telescope were able to measure the age of our universe, to detect ancient galaxies in their different stages of development, and to gather mountains of data about the atmosphere and composition of other planets outside our solar system. A new telescope to replace the Hubble was launched in 2013. It orbits at a greater

---

4. Peterson, *Christ Plays in Ten Thousand Places*, 123.

distance from the earth and is even more powerful. Albert Einstein, the great scientist, has this to say: "The most beautiful experience we can have is the mysterious ... Whoever does not know it and can no longer wonder, no longer marvel, is as good as dead, and his eyes are diminished."[5]

The spiritual life needs it. The spiritual life, without wonder, cannot grow and is stunted. Wonder requires us to be open to the mysteries around us. With no room for mysteries, we approach life based on predictable outcomes and critical analysis in search of measurable objectives. We look and scan for information in order to master and gain control over our life and environment. Life without wonder, as Eugene Peterson laments, is a self-help project and spiritual formation is reduced to cosmetics.[6] The spiritual life, without wonder or mystery, is shallow and artificial. It lacks depth and authenticity. As Paul says, it has an outward form of godliness but lacking the power within.

## Seeing Beyond the Ordinary

Someone put up these words near the door to the chapel. Those who enter the chapel will take notice of what it says:

> God shows Godself everywhere,
> 
> In everything,
> 
> In people and in things and in nature and in events.
> 
> It becomes very obvious that God is everywhere and
> 
> in everything and we cannot be without God
> 
> It is impossible.
> 
> The only thing is that we don't see it.[7]

Why don't we see it if God is everywhere and in everything? A story is told that a fish spent all its life trying to figure out a mystery called "ocean". It asked for an answer but nobody knew

---

5. Einstein, *Ideas and Opinions*, 11.
6. Peterson, *Christ Plays*, 123.
7. De Waal, "Attentiveness" 22.

about this mystery named "ocean". The fish finally concluded that there was no such thing called "ocean". It had looked everywhere and spent its life swimming in many places and directions and still did not know what this "ocean" was about. How could it believe in something that could not be seen and described by anyone?[8] Sometimes we are like the fish in this story. God, like the "ocean" in the story, gives us life and our existence depends on him. He, like the ocean, is around us all the time and yet we do not see him. We conclude that we cannot see God because he cannot be found.

A blind man begged Jesus to heal him of his blindness in the eighth chapter of the Gospel of Mark. Jesus took the man outside the village, spit on his eyes, and put his hands on him asking, "Do you see anything?" The blind man replied saying that he saw people like trees walking around. Jesus then put his hands on his eyes and this time his sight was restored. He saw everything clearly. This story is placed alongside an earlier event when Jesus chided his disciples for having eyes but not see (Mark 8:18). This took place when the disciples were with Jesus on a boat. They had witnessed the miracle of Jesus feeding the four thousand with seven loaves of bread and a few small fish before crossing the lake on a boat to the other side. In the boat the disciples realized their mistake. They brought along only one loaf of bread which was not enough for all of them. Perhaps this matter weighed heavily on their minds when Jesus talked to them to watch out for the yeast of the Pharisees and Herod. When they disciples heard the word "yeast" they jumped to the conclusion that Jesus was talking about not having enough bread in the boat! They had not looked beyond ordinary bread to the one who was the Bread of life. Soon after the feeding of the five thousand, Jesus declared that those who came to him would never be hungry and those who believed in him would never be thirsty (John 6:35).

---

8. Story adapted from Silf's *Companions of Christ*, 17–18.

How then do we begin to see the world from a different perspective? According to Merton, this is not possible without Christ. He wrote:

> God is everywhere. Truth and love pervade all things as the light and heat of the sun pervade our atmosphere. But just as the rays of the sun do not set fire to anything by themselves, so God does not touch our souls with the fire of the supernatural knowledge and experience without Christ.[9]

Jesus was referring to the corrupt and evil disposition of these people when he talked about the yeast of the Pharisees and Herod. A corrupt heart will never be able to see God in the ordinary things of everyday life. Jesus said that only the pure in heart can see God (Matt 5:8). A pure heart, transformed by Christ's love through obedience to him, has the capacity to wonder. "Wonder," according to Abraham Heschel, "is the well spring of love."[10]

## The Ordinary Permeated by the Divine

We are able to see the ordinary permeated by the divine with the eyes of wonder. What do we see when we look at the birds of the air and the flowers of the field? Do we marvel at how the birds are able to gather food so freely without a care in the world? Birds do not fall from the sky because they lack food. They survive because God, through the abundance in nature, feeds them. We admire the flowers of the field for their exquisite shape and beauty. They are dressed better than all the garments in the world even though they do not work or spin. Do we see the glory of God shining through these flowers of the field? Jesus challenged his disciples to change the way they viewed the world. He challenges us not just to look at the birds and flowers as inanimate objects. He wants us to see them as creatures loved and cared for by the Creator God. We must learn to respond to the divine presence percolating through the created world.

---

9. Merton, *New Seeds of Contemplation*, 151.
10. Dresner, *I Asked for Wonder*, 2–3.

I chased away the starlings that came to perch on the roof just outside the window of my daughter's room. The small birds were black in color with red eyes. They were not pleasant to the eyes. I considered them a nuisance for soiling the place with their droppings. I preferred watching the high flying eagles that circled above my apartment. They flew with strength and grace and always looking for potential prey in the sea below. One day a thought crossed my mind. Weren't these little birds loved and cared by God? He fed and took care of them. They were his creatures and part of his wonderful creation. I was questioning the work of his hands if I despised these creatures. This outlook changed my attitude towards these birds. I began to like them for what they were without making any judgment or analysis. I stepped back in wonder instead of trying to control the starlings.

## Seeing with Eyes of Faith

Paul prays for the Ephesian Christians that the eyes of their heart may be open and see. Sight is based on what we see with our physical eyes. Faith is necessary for us to see with the eyes of our heart. We need faith to believe that God is around and hidden in the ordinary things of everyday life since he is invisible to our eyes. We can see beyond what we normally perceive with the eyes of faith. We believe that God is everywhere and the world is charged with his divine presence.

Fear stifles our faith. We are fearful of losing control. Conversely, faith is yielding control to the God whom we trust. I shooed the birds away fearing that they would pollute the roof with their droppings. I did not see the birds with eyes of faith. Jesus reprimanded the disciples for their fear in not having enough loaves of bread in the boat. It was fear that caused them to misunderstand Jesus' words. They should look beyond the physical bread to the one who was the Bread of Life. They should look beyond their physical hunger to the person who could satisfy their spiritual hunger and thirst for Jesus said that "he who comes to me will never go hungry, and he who believes in me will never be thirsty"(John 6:35). It was not surprising that when the disciples saw Jesus walking on water or stilling the storm they were filled with terror instead of wonder. Jesus reprimanded them for lacking faith.

Sue Monk Kidd writes that if we want to see the fingerprints of God in this world, we must learn to look at something and see beyond the ordinary. It will be hidden from us unless we look for it. She writes: "With eyes of faith we can begin now to discover the holiness, the sign, hidden in each common thing, the reality and love of God all around us, by deciding to look for it."[11]

## Seeing with Heart of Humility

Humility, besides faith, is needed to see the world with wonder. Humility means to suspend judgment and let what is before us to reveal itself on its own terms. To David Rensberger, the spiritual life has always been about living small: having less, being less visible, and less known. Humility is needed to live the authentic spiritual life. One way to nurture humility is the spiritual discipline of attentiveness to small things. He is referring to the world of small things designed and loved by God that lies underneath our feet that we hardly notice. We need to slow down our pace, lower our height, bend down on our knees, and put our faces close to the ground to observe the world of small things. Interestingly, the ground or "humus" is where the word "humble" is derived. We will discover, for the first time, a tiny universe filled with fascinating things when we slow down and take time to observe the small world below us.[12]

Talking about humility, it is good to note that a child sees things at ground level. An adult has the advantage of "height" due to years of experience behind him. His knowledge and experience tell him a cloud is made up of tiny water droplets so light that they float in the air. A child has no knowledge of this. So she cannot judge clouds based on her knowledge or experience. She uses her imagination. She sees not just a cloud of tiny water droplets.

---

11. Kidd, *God's Joyful Surprise*, 152.
12. Rensberger, "The Heaven Below" 44.

# THE GIFT OF WONDER

She sees faces, animals, and all kinds of objects in the clouds. The child sees the unique form in terms of individuals and personalities while the adult sees the general form. To an adult, an oak tree is an oak tree and nothing more. One oak tree is no different from another oak tree for they belong to the same kind. Each tree, for a child, is different with its own unique characteristics. We all know that knowledge can make us proud. It can prevent us from seeing things that are beyond our expectation. One day the disciples of Jesus wanted to know who was the greatest in the kingdom of heaven. Jesus took a little child and made him stand in their midst. He said:

> I tell you the truth, unless you change and become like little children, you will never enter the kingdom of heaven. Therefore, whoever humbles himself like this child is the greatest in the kingdom of heaven (Matt 18:3–4).

## Seeing with a Thankful Heart

We also need a thankful heart to see the world with wonder. Paul calls on us to give thanks in everything and that includes the wonderful world around us. We have an innate tendency to control and possess the things we see. Gratitude will help us to overcome this tendency. To be thankful is to view the world as a gift from the Creator. Usually we scan the horizon with the purpose of extracting information. We are able to exert control and possession over our environment with the information we gather. Seeing with a thankful heart is a "kind of graced vision that is focused more on receiving gifts" that can help us to see the world differently.[13]

One day a pilgrim was walking under a dark stormy sky when he came across a small field of ripe wheat in the valley just below him. The patch of field, under a darkening sky, was a perfect picture of brightness swaying gently in the wind. The pilgrim was enjoying this beautiful sight as he walked the path that led to the valley below him. Not long he met a farmer coming in the opposite

---

13. Paintner, "Cultivating the Eyes of the Heart" 29.

direction. He was returning home with downcast eyes after a hard day's work. The pilgrim stopped him and patting his arms gently said, "Thank you." The farmer was surprised by this gesture and said, "I have nothing to give to you, why do you thank me?" The pilgrim replied with a smile, "I am not thanking you to make you give me something. You have cared for that square of wheat, and through your labor it has acquired the beauty it has today . . . I've been walking, and all the way I have been nourished by its golden color." The farmer was indeed surprised by the pilgrim's comment.[14]

## Expecting the Unexpected

We must also be willing to be surprised. I was taking some students on a mission trip to the interior of Sarawak, East Malaysia. We were ministering to the Ibans: an indigenous group who lived in long houses. The building on stilts had a long common corridor that housed many families. The Ibans are communal people who love to share and socialize. Some of the families still have human skulls hanging on the beams just outside their doors. The Ibans were former headhunters. The place we stayed had no electricity. The generators worked only for a couple of hours at night in order to save diesel. The place was completely dark by nine o'clock in the night. The people woke up early in the morning before dawn to work.

We slept outside on the common corridor. The air was cool and we could smell the fumes coming from the mosquito coils. The place was dead quiet and the only sound came from the noise made by the insects in the forest. Our greatest worry was the merciless mosquitoes looking for fresh blood. Suddenly at a distance, we saw a solitary tree filled with bright lights. We were wondering what it was. The area was completely dark and there was no artificial lights around the place. The roof above us was suddenly filled with a myriad of colored lights. Our longhouse was invaded by hundreds of fireflies! It was an amazing sight that we would not forget. This came as a surprise to us.

14. Gros, *A Philosophy of Walking*, 56.

## THE GIFT OF WONDER

In order to increase the moments of awareness, Esther de Waal, who has written on Benedictine and Celtic spiritualities, suggests using a magnifying glass for walks around the neighborhood. She will walk slowly, stopping and looking at whatever that catches her attention: a leaf, a stone, a twig or whatever comes to her hand. Using her magnifying glass she is surprised by a whole other world seen in a moss or weeds that creep through the cracks of pavements. This is what she has to say:

> Time and again the glass has brought me a sharp shock of surprise, sometimes so intense that I have cried out in wonder and amazement. Surprise is one of God's best gifts . . . I see patterns and configurations, endlessly delicate and different—a diversity of shape and form that carries a harmony and a relatedness of the parts to the whole. I see a glimpse of this mysterious inter-relatedness, a glimpse of the mystery at the heart of the universe.[15]

Most of the time we are not surprised by what we see because we shut up those things that we do not expect to see. We are looking for or processing information from what we see rather than really seeing. We must be open to see the unexpected if we want surprises. Mary Magdalene went to the tomb of Jesus expecting to see his body and hoping to anoint it with spices. The first attempt was done in haste because of the coming Sabbath. The tomb's door was opened and Jesus' body was not there. She became hysterical and cried thinking that someone had taken the Lord's body and not knowing where they had put him. She did not expect to see a risen Jesus. She did not realize that it was Jesus standing behind her when she turned around. She assumed that he was the gardener. She was able to recognize her beloved Lord only when Jesus called out her name. She went back with the news saying, "I have seen the Lord!"

---

15. De Waal, "Attentiveness" 27.

# Take Up Your Mat and Walk

## Ordinary Miracles Everywhere

We are easily astonished and surprised by extraordinary events like Jesus rising from the dead, the changing of water into wine, or Aaron's rod that budded. Events like these happen only once and they are not everyday occurrences. Everyday babies are being born and yet few wonder at the miracle of birth. Trees sprouted from the earth and we hardly notice them. We marvel at the feeding of the five thousand and yet we hardly think of the seeds of grain sown and grow into full ears ready for harvesting to feed millions. We are amazed at the miracle of water turning to wine. Wendell Berry considers this a small miracle compared with the greater and still continuing miracle "by which water (with soil and sunlight) is fumed into grapes." He goes on to say that holiness cannot be confined for "holiness is everywhere in Creation, it is as common as raindrops and leaves and blades of grass."[16]

We are surrounded by wonders everywhere. Miracles not captured by the naked eye are happening around us all the time. The glory of God is mediated through the physical world. God has given us two books in order for us to know and love him. We marvel at the many miraculous events taking place in human history when we read the Bible. The other book is the Book of Nature. This book cannot be confined in a classroom for debate or discussion. It has to be read outdoors. We too are confronted with the mysteries and miracles of life reading this book. We have to read this book with the lens of faith, humility, gratitude, and the willingness to be surprised. Berry thinks that the Bible should be read outdoors as well. Augustine agrees saying that when he reads outside, he is engaging two books at once. The texts of Scripture and Nature compliment each other. Both reveal the mysteries of God using different modes of discourse. They allow for a greater display of the imagination and interpretation.[17] Someone asked Saint Antony how he was able to live the spiritual life without access to the holy books. He replied,

---

16. Berry, "Christianity and the Survival of Creation" 149.
17. Lane, *Backpacking*, 229.

"My book is the nature of created things and any time I want to read the words of God the book is there before me."[18]

## Wonder Captured through the Lens

One way to read the Book of Nature is the use of a camera. Christine Paintner is a photographer and writer. She shares that photography can be used to deepen awareness and love in her book *Eyes of the Heart: Photography as a Christian Contemplative Practice.* According to her, creative photography used contemplatively can transform the way we view the world. Normally we use a camera to scan our field of vision for information or the things we want to see. We are looking for some spectacular scenes, fascinating or beautiful objects to take photos. Instead of taking photos, she suggests that we should be open to receive them as gifts offered to us. If we are willing to see the world differently with a camera, we will have this profound awareness that life is an unending stream of gifts.[19] She has this advice for those of us who are keen on using photography as a contemplative practice:

> Try this next time you feel overcome by beauty—pause there as long as you can without moving to do something else or complete another task. And then, when there is a sense of fullness or completion, pick up a camera or a pen, and allow them to become the tools to honor what you have experienced and your expression of deep gratitude. Rather than "capturing" the encounter, let this be a prayer, so that slowly over time you might find yourself in an unending litany of praise.[20]

We know that Thomas Merton viewed things differently from most people based on the photos that he took. He would take photos of an old fence, weeds growing between cracks, working gloves on a stool, a dead root, or a broken stone wall instead of beautiful objects, people or scenery. Merton was not searching

---

18. Ibid., 229.
19. Paintner, "Cultivating the Eyes of the Heart" 29–30.
20. Ibid., 31.

for something to photograph. He allowed whatever that crossed his path to present itself. He gave each item his attention without imposing on them. He allowed each to speak on its own terms and to have its own voice.[21] Once Merton reprimanded a fellow photographer for the way he approached things with his camera. He told him to stop looking and to begin seeing:

> Because looking means that you have something in mind for your eye to find; you've set out in search of your desired object and have closed off everything else presenting itself along the way. But seeing is being open and receptive to what comes to the eye; your vision total and not targeted.[22]

The world made by God is full of wonders. How we view the world depends on the lens of our heart. We need the lens of faith, humility, and thankfulness to view the world with wonder. It is not only good for the human spirit but for the spiritual life as well to develop a sense of wonder. Our spiritual life is shallow and superficial without a sense of wonder. We approach life based on careful analysis and predictable outcomes. This kind of spirituality is based on acquiring the right information and techniques. It lacks authenticity and is manipulative. With a sense of wonder we are able to see the glory of God embedded in the ordinary things of life. God's presence becomes real to us everywhere we go. We live the spiritual life expecting the unexpected and looking to God to surprise us.

When we begin seeing the things around us with wonder, we are actually giving them our attention without imposing on them. We allow each to speak with its own voice. For this to happen we need to create a hospitable space in our hearts to receive without seeking anything in return. This is made possible by God's love in us. The love of God replaces fear in our hearts. The space is often squeezed out due to fear. The fears of rejection, failure, ridicule, and shame make it impossible for us to open a space in our

21. De Waal, *Lost in Wonder*, 64.
22. Seitz, *Song for Nobody*, 133–34.

hearts for others. To receive a stranger, for the early Christians, is to welcome Christ. They had replaced the fear for strangers with their faith in Christ. Extending hospitality even to strangers had become a virtue of the early Church that even the pagans could unreservedly testify.

## Questions for Reflection and Discussion

1. How have science and technology stripped you of your sense of wonder?
2. What cause you to lose your childhood sense of wonder? How can you regain back this childhood wonder?
3. Why is a sense of wonder necessary to your spiritual life?
4. What are needed to see the world with wonder? What is the difference between looking and seeing according to Merton? How can this help you to see the world differently?

## Chapter 6

# THE HOSPITABLE SPACE

I was a stranger and you invited me in.

—JESUS CHRIST[1]

Hospitality is the creation of a free space where the stranger can enter and become a friend.

—HENRI NOUWEN[2]

### Christian Hospitality as Welcoming Christ

JESUS GAVE THE REASON why he welcomed the sheep, and not the goats, into his Kingdom (Matt 25:31–46). They gave him something to eat and drink when he was hungry and thirsty. They invited him to their homes even though he was a stranger. They clothed him when he needed clothes. They looked after him when he was sick. They came to visit him when he was in prison. The righteous asked how did all these be possible. Jesus went on to explain that they did these to him when they did all these to the least of his people. The statement by Jesus, "I was a stranger and you welcomed me", set the stage for Christians to view Christian hospitality as welcoming Christ in their midst. Hospitality has,

---

1. Matt 25: 35.
2. Nouwen, *Reaching Out*, 51.

## THE HOSPITABLE SPACE

since then, become a trademark of the Christian's identity and a touchstone of his spirituality. Chrysostom, the archbishop of Constantinople in the fourth century, instructed his people to set up a guestroom in their house with a bed, table, and candlestick. The special room was to welcome guests. It was to be a Christ's cell, set apart for him.[3]

The early Church took hospitality seriously. We see evidence of this in the writings of the apostles. Paul called on believers to practice hospitality by sharing with God's people who had needs (Rom 12:13). Peter encouraged his readers to offer hospitality to one another without grumbling (1 Pet 4:9). John commented his dear friend, Gaius, for showing hospitality to those brothers who worked for the truth even though they were strangers to him. He wrote: "You do well to send them on their way in a manner worthy of God. It was for the sake of the Name that they went out, receiving no help from the pagans. We ought therefore to show hospitality to such men so that we may work together for the truth" (3 John 6–8).

The hospitality of the Christians following the apostolic age even took the Roman emperor Julian by surprise. Julian who was anti-Christian had this to say: "The godless Galileans fed not only their poor but ours also." According to Tertullian, the father of Latin Christianity, even pagans confessed that the Christians truly loved one another. The groups of people that were cared by believers included burying the poor, supplying the needs of boys and girls who were deprived, helping the elderly who were too weak to leave their homes, providing for those who suffered shipwreck, and gave to those who were banished to hard labor in mines or islands for their faith in Christ.[4]

Christine Pohl in *Making Room* points out several aspects confronting the early Church that made hospitality the centerpiece of her Christian practice.[5] Cultural differences between the Gentile and Jewish believers and the social differences between the rich and poor made the sharing of meals together a real challenge. The hospitality

---

3. Chrysostom, "Homily 45 on Acts" 277.
4. Foster, *Freedom of Simplicity*, 62–63.
5. Pohl, *Making Room*, 32.

of sharing meals in such contexts portrayed the common life of believers based on mutual respect, recognition, and equality. Believers traveled far and wide to spread the Gospel. Hospitality granted to the early missionaries and church leaders played a crucial role in the work of the Kingdom. The church worshiped in the homes of the believers. It was natural to practice hospitality when believers met together in a family-like atmosphere. In the light of these, it was a reasonable demand for the leadership in the early Church to exercise the gift of hospitality (1 Tim 3:2; Titus 1:8). Women played an important role in hospitality. It was required for widows who were put on the list for church support to show evidence of hospitality as part of their good deeds (1 Tim 5:9-10).

The welcoming of strangers as guests was given a strong emphasis under the Rule of Benedict in the sixth century:

> All guest who present themselves are to be welcomed as Christ, for himself will say: "I was a stranger and you welcomed me" (Matt 25:35). Once a guest has been announced, the superior and the community are to meet the guest with all the courtesy of love. First of all, they are to pray together and thus be united in peace ... Great care and concern are to be shown in receiving the poor people and pilgrims, because in them more particularly Christ is received; our very awe of the rich guarantees them special respect.[6]

## Hospitality Celebrated in the "Holy Trinity"

This theme of Christian hospitality was celebrated in a famous masterpiece called "Holy Trinity" by a monk named Andrei Rublev in 1411 A.D. This icon, depicting harmony and accord, was painted during a period of trouble and discord in Russian history. Icons are used to address the troublesome questions of the day. Each period in history has their peculiar and distinctive problems and the subjects of icons reflect these circumstances. The subject

---

6. Rule of Benedict 53:1; 3-4; 15. See Chittister, *Wisdom Distilled from the Daily*, 121.

of Rublev's icon focuses on the biblical story of the three angels who disguise themselves as travelers. They are enjoying the hospitality of the patriarch Abraham under the shady trees of Mamre. Sarah and Abraham are deliberately left out in the painting. The background of the icon has pictures of a stylized oak, a building depicting Abraham's house, and a mountain.

The focus is shifted from the biblical event in order to underline its theological significance. In this painting, Rublev is projecting a vision of accord and peace made by the three Persons of the Godhead: Father, Son, and Holy Spirit. Like all icons, the purpose is to draw the viewer into the story of the painting and to become part of the scene. The three angelic figures have their heads inclined toward each other in an endless, silent conversation. A circular, hospitable space is formed among them. The centerpiece of this space is the Eucharist cup that invites the viewer to share in the hosts' welcome. This welcome is made possible by the outpouring of love for many through the sacrifice of Christ.

## Hospitality Around Meals

The Lord's Supper was enacted during a meal. The sharing of food is the primary act of hospitality in most human cultures. When we were walking in an ancient village in China we met an old woman who invited us to her home to have tea with her. It was a typical rural Chinese house with a huge courtyard. All the rooms faced the courtyard, including the dining, living, kitchen, and store room. She was taking care of her grandchild for her daughter-in-law who was a teacher in a nearby school. She again invited us to stay for lunch when her daughter-in-law came back from school for her lunch break. It was difficult to reject her kindness. She gave us a bag of pickled chilies as a parting gift before we left her place. She treated us like old friends though we were complete strangers to her. We left the village grateful for the kind reception we received.

The first recorded human act of hospitality in the Bible is when Abraham invited the three men to his tent for a meal. He did not know that they were angels of the Lord. It is for this reason that the author to the book of Hebrews calls on us to "entertain strangers for by doing so some people have entertained angels without knowing it"(Heb 13:2). God's acts of hospitality are clearly shown in creation and redemption. In the creation story he invited Adam and Eve to his garden filled with delightful trees and edible fruits. He called on the first couple to eat from what they could get in the garden. He also invites us to partake of the cup and bread during the time of communion. God's gift of salvation has been extended to us. Each time we observe communion we are reminded to give thanks and cherish this gift of hospitality in our hearts. In return, we need to extend hospitality to others whom we can share this gift from God.

It is interesting to note that during the course of Jesus' earthly ministry he was invited for meals by all kinds of people. Jesus not only having meals with them, but he also told stories revolving around meals. The hospitality expressed through sharing a meal together provides the ideal setting for welcoming Jesus into our midst. The hospitality of daily meals with friends, family, and guests and graced by Jesus' presence "are the most natural and frequent settings for working out the personal and social implications of salvation"[7]

### Room in the Heart

It is not enough that we share a meal or spare a bed for our guests. As a Danish proverb says, "If there is room in the heart, there is room in the house." Marjorie Thompson in *Soul Feast* gives a good definition of biblical hospitality.

> Hospitality means receiving the other, from the heart, into my own dwelling place. It entails providing for the need, comfort, and delight of the other with all the openness, respect, freedom, tenderness, and joy that love itself embodies.[8]

---

7. Peterson, *Christ Plays in Ten Thousand Places*, 214.
8. Thompson, *Soul Feast*, 122.

## THE HOSPITABLE SPACE

Hospitality from the heart is an expression of God's love inside us. We love because God loves us. We extend this love to others by inviting them into our own dwelling places. A dwelling place can mean a physical place. It can also mean a "space" in our hearts for others. Is there room in our hearts for others "to play, question, and converse; room to be heard and understood; room to reveal themselves as they choose?"[9]

We know that physical space can affect us emotionally. Some experience agoraphobia: the fear of open or public places. They prefer to stay at home to avoid the panic of being out in the open. Others suffer from claustrophobia: the fear of crowded spaces. Going into a crowded lift with little elbow room to spare can cause a sense of panic or suffocation to the sufferer. Physical space can have a psychological effect on our behavior as well. We withdraw into our own private spot when we find ourselves in a crowded space. We close our minds to the people and things around us. We behave differently in an open field. We begin to open up by allowing our feelings and ideas to get through us. The experience with physical space has parallels in the social realm. Emotionally and mentally, we may feel our space being squeezed and boxed in by unhealthy competition, unreasonable deadlines, or high expectations. We can become impatient and intolerant. Conversely, we become alive and energized when we are given the space to move due to the acceptance, appreciation, and cooperation by others.[10]

### Creating Space for Others

Hospitality, according to Nouwen, is the creation of a free space where others can feel free to be themselves. It is not to change people or to win them to our side, but to provide them a space where change can take place.[11] We need to take note of the cluttered room in our hearts before we can create a space for others. We have difficulty tolerating an empty space in our hearts. If our hearts are

---

9. Ibid., 122.
10. Palmer, *To Know as We are Known*, 70.
11. Nouwen, *Reaching Out*, 71.

not occupied with things to do, we feel restless. At the same time we become preoccupied or worry over the things we hope to do. Occupations and preoccupations will clutter our hearts and prevent us from creating a space for others. Jean Vanier, founder of an international network of communities for people with intellectual disabilities, made this confession. He said that, at times, when he invited people to his office to talk, he was busy and had to attend to other things. He wrote, "The door of my office is opened, but the door of my heart was closed."[12] There was no room in his heart for others because he was occupied and preoccupied with his own thoughts and busyness.

We need solitude to open the door of our hearts. Solitude shields us from external concerns so that we can begin to take note of the thoughts and worries that clutter our hearts. The spiritual practice of solitude, which will be discussed in the next chapter, frees us from the compulsions of the false self. The false self compels us to seek control, security, and affection. We are free to deal with the authentic self in a truthful manner when we are no longer nagged by the compulsions of the false self. Our hospitality may be wrongly motivated if we are not careful. We can be motivated by a need for approval or to exercise power, even spiritual power, over others.[13] Our hospitality based on love has to be authentic which only the true self can give. Social etiquette requires us to put on a smile to our guests even when our hearts and minds are blocked by worry or seeking to control. Alan Jones is right when he says that sometimes we love out of the inner cravings for control, security, and affection. These cravings masquerade as love, but they are counterfeits.[14]

Our guests carry gifts in return for our hospitality when we play host to them. The angels revealed to Abraham that Sarah would give birth to a son when he played host to the them at Mamre. Jesus offered himself to Mary and Martha when they invited him to their home. Mary was able to enjoy his company

12. Vanier, *Community and Growth*, 267.
13. Vanier, *Becoming Human*, 109.
14. Jones, *Soul Making*, 132.

## THE HOSPITABLE SPACE

by listening to the master. Jesus revealed himself to the two disciples through the breaking of bread when they invited him to their home. A Benedictine monk must also be willing to receive whatever the guest may teach him when he provides hospitality to him or her. He does not asked, out of a sense of superiority, that the guest needs to conform to a set of beliefs or the social milieu. The monk usually greets the guest with the words, "Your blessing please" which means "I am glad you are here; I recognize Christ in you; I am ready to receive what you have to offer; I welcome you to this place to share our life."[15] Jesus asked the woman for a favor when he met her at the well. He asked her for a drink for he was thirsty. This act of hospitality by Jesus opened a door of hope for the woman and others in the community.

On a different occasion, Jesus again, through an act of hospitality, opened a door of hope to a woman in distress. We are familiar with the story about Jesus going to Jairus' house to attend to his dying daughter upon his urgent request. The crowd that was with Jesus sensed the urgency and they followed closely by pressing behind him. In the crowd was a woman who suffered from a blood disease for a long time. She too needed healing from Jesus. She also knew that Jesus had no time for her. She decided to sneak from behind and touch the cloak of the busy rabbi instead of seeking an audience with him. She reasoned that by touching his cloak she could be healed. What happened next caught her by surprise. Jesus stopped and asked for the person who touched his cloak. He wanted to attend to this woman's difficulties. He had an urgent matter at hand and was not required to pay heed to this woman's woes. The urgent matter had to wait.

He stopped and created a space for this woman to tell her story. She was fearful not knowing what would happen to her when she came forward to identify herself. Her fears were laid to rest when she saw Jesus because he looked at her with eyes of compassion. She knew in her heart that Jesus was there to listen to her story. He would share her pain without judgment and prejudice. In the hospitable space given by Jesus she began to have the freedom

---

15. Canham, "A School for the Lord's Service" 18.

and courage to tell her painful story. Telling the truth enabled her to confront her suffering and fears that lodged in her heart for a long time. Jesus consoled her with these words, "Daughter, your faith has healed you. Go in peace and be freed from your suffering" (Mark 5:35). A change had occurred in that hospitable space offered by Jesus to the woman. She had shalom. Healing had gone beyond the physical condition to her whole person. She not only enjoyed good health but also a healthy relationship with herself, others, and God.

## Hospitality in Different Worlds

We belong to different worlds. We move in and out of different relationships all the time. Part of our being human, as Jean Vanier points out, is that we cannot live in a solitary state. We need to connect, out of mutual dependency, with others and learn to belong.[16] The home, school, and workplace are the different worlds that we belong on a daily basis. We can carve out a hospitable space for our children, guests, students, and colleagues in these places.[17]

## Hospitality at Home

Children, who are treated as guests in the home, need a safe and secure place to grow up. The home should be a hospitable place, but unfortunately this is not the case in many homes. Many children come from broken homes. Conflict and strife have squeezed out the space needed for wholesome and healthy growth. A hospitable environment is needed to equip them with the characteristic traits of wisdom, strength, and freedom. They need these traits to stand against an inhospitable world out there. A blessed home, according to the Bible, is where children are trained as "polished arrows" to shoot straight and to contend with the enemies at the gate (Ps 127:4–5). A hospitable space is a safe place where children can

---

16. Vanier, *Becoming Human*, 41.

17. Material in this section is taken from my book, *Being Truly Human*, 69–75.

grow and develop without the fear of criticism and rejection. It is a non-threatening place where children feel secure enough to ask the wrong questions and make mistakes. The home is not a place without boundaries. A safe and secure place needs fencing. The child needs to be protected from harm while enjoying the space. The child must know what he can and cannot do. Setting limits will help the child curb with his appetites and desires. This will develop his character and teach him to respect the space of others.

## Hospitality at School

Some years ago my wife tutored a child who hated school. He loved animals and his favorite was the lion. He had a toy lion at home that he named Alex. He considered Alex a close buddy and liked talking to him all the time. One day my wife asked him to draw a picture that he liked. He drew a lion eating up a man. The drawing shocked my wife. She asked who was the man in the picture. He told her that the man was a teacher in his school. Many of us can recall some painful experiences with teachers at school. We were fearful of our teachers when we were young and naive. They looked like giants to us. We called them by all sorts of names based on our perceptions of them. In primary school I had a physical education teacher who intimidated us on the first day of class. He liked to instill fear on his students. He took a huge ruler and whacked it hard on a desk in front of him in order to frighten the students. He put fear in our hearts by saying that he would not hesitate to use his "weapon" on anyone who disobeyed his marching orders. His ploy worked perfectly. The students did not give him much trouble in all his classes. We dislike school because such teachers can make life difficult for us. Once a while, we meet a teacher we like because her presence does not intimidate us. She has given us a space in our hearts to grow and develop. She is someone that we remember for as long as we live.

Parker Palmer, who wrote extensively on the spiritual formation of education, warns that words used by teachers can close up the learning space because students do not want to reveal their ignorance and be embarrassed before their peers.[18] A hospitable space is needed for students to learn well without fear or intimidation, Unfortunately this is not happening in the schools in East Asia. The concept that the teacher knows best is common in many cultures. Teachers are quick to offer answers to problems raised in order to prove their authority and expertise. Some teachers do not encourage meaningful discourse in order to maintain their invincibility in class. The learning process is always one sided. Boundaries are set to make sure this happens. Students will be penalized if they step over the line. The "good" students are those who toe the line in order to please the teacher. The more adventurous students who prefer to throw in their own ideas are penalized. This style of teaching will not open up a learning space for students to learn and obey truth.

## Hospitality at Work

Henry Ford, the renowned American pioneer in mass production using the assembly line strategy, liked to make this complaint: how is it that he always has to engage a man or a woman when all he needs is a pair of hands? He will have his wish fulfilled if he is alive today. The robotic arm in car factories takes over the pair of human hands. The question reveals that companies, by and large, show interest not in the worker as a person but in the bottom line: productivity and profitability. The worker, if he is not productive, can be easily replaced like cogs in a machine. Fortunately humans are not machines. They can get sick and have moods. They can also lead, innovate, create, love, serve, and hate. William Pollard, the chairman of Service-Master, makes this observation:

> But people have the potential to improve upon their knowledge, to modify, to adapt, and to exercise judgment within a framework of moral values. It is not just what we are doing, but what we are becoming in the process that gives us distinct value and is uniquely human.[19]

---

18. Palmer, *To Know As We Are Known*, 74.
19. Pollard, *The Soul of the Firm*, 26.

## THE HOSPITABLE SPACE

Pollard's firm is committed not only to excellence and profitability but also to people development. A hospitable space is created for the worker to grow and develop his potential. It is a space where commitment goes both ways. The worker is committed to giving quality work for his company and the firm is committed to the welfare and growth of its workers. Both, through their commitments, are adding value to each other. Pollard's firm finds out that the employee tends to be more loyal and committed to the company where the environment favors the worker.

Max DePree, chairman of a furniture company, sees the need to recognize and tap the full potential of his workers. In his acclaimed book, *Leadership is an Art*, he notes that a leader should be able to liberate people to do what is required of them in the most effective and humane way. For example, each worker in his firm who has an idea to contribute should be taken seriously. Leaders, who endorse the concept that people have different gifts, talent, and skills, are trained to listen carefully and respond to the followers creatively. Each worker is unique and can play an important role in the company. Leaders should have the confidence to "encourage contrary opinions," and "to abandon themselves to the strength of others."[20]

Most of us view work in purely remunerative terms. The parable of the vineyard workers will give us a different perspective on work. In the parable, the early batch of workers receive the same salary as the last batch that work only for one hour. The early batch of workers who work for money are not happy with this arrangement. They think they deserve to be paid more for the hours they work in comparison to the last batch. The last batch are happy that they can find work at the last hour. They stand the whole day, under the hot sun, waiting to be employed. For them, work gives dignity. The owner of the vineyard pays all the workers the same salary to bring home the point: work that makes use of a person's gifts and potential is what makes him truly human. Hospitality, in the workplace, requires us to treat people with respect and dignity.

20. DePree, *Leadership is an Art*, xx.

# Take Up Your Mat and Walk

## Hospitality to the Marginalized

My wife worked at a center for homeschoolers. The children would come to the center to be supervised in their school work. The supervisors were there to make sure they finished the assigned work for the day and to help them in their school work. This center was different from the normal schools because it allowed each student to learn at his or her own pace. It was not unusual to have a mixed group of students, with different age groups and learning levels, to be in the same class. Some students, who were marginalized by the mainstream because of learning disabilities, found a home at the center. The church-run center maintained a policy of inclusion by taking in autistic and slow learners. The mainstream schools did not cater to people who lived at the fringe.

The marginalized and downtrodden are considered misfits in mainstream society. Why does society at large exclude these people? Jean Vanier, who found L'Arche, contends that the root cause of this prejudice is fear.[21] There are several reasons for this fear. If society includes them, the people fear that this will upset their lifestyle, cost them time and money, affect their social status, and draw criticism from friends and relatives. Hence few people will want to take this risk to include the marginalized in our society.

If fear excludes these people, then trust is needed to open a space in the hearts for the marginalized. Trust is not easily available because from a young age we learn mostly through fear. The fear of rejection keeps us wanting to please others. The fear of failure makes us competitive and wanting to succeed. The fear of ridicule forbids us from taking risks. The fear of shame prevents us from opening up our lives to others. We begin to see the marginalized differently when we learn to overcome these fears and open a hospitable space in our hearts for such people. We realize that they are people like us with genuine needs. Their fears reveal our fears; their weaknesses reflect our vulnerability; their frustration speaks to our frustration.

---

21. Vanier, *Becoming Human*, 73.

## THE HOSPITABLE SPACE

When I read the Scripture, I begin to see that God gauges our spirituality not primarily on how much we spend time in prayer, how well we do the disciplines, how many ministries we serve in the church, or how many souls we won to Christ, but on how much we include the marginalized and downtrodden in our life. Many times Jesus ministered to people on the fringe: the woman with a blood disease; social outcasts like the leper, the lame, the blind, and the dumb; the Samaritan woman; the demon-possessed; tax-collectors; woman caught in adultery; and many more. The prophet Isaiah, knowing that the worshipers' hearts were not open to those in distress, cried out when he saw them going to the temple to fast and offered sacrifices:

> Is not this the kind of fasting I have chosen: to loose the chains of injustice and untie the cords of the yoke, to set the oppressed free and break every yoke? Is it not to share your food with the hungry and to provide the poor wanderer with shelter—when you see the naked, to clothe him, and not to turn away from your own flesh and blood? (Isa 58:6–7).

⸺

Hospitality is a Christian virtue exemplified by our Lord Jesus. Everywhere he went he found time and space to minister to people from all walks of life. Particular attention was given to the poor, downtrodden, and the marginalized. This habit had been practiced for many centuries by the Christians but has lost much of its shine today. This is clearly seen in many churches on a Sunday morning. A stranger that comes to church may be officially welcomed during the announcements but easily left alone after the service is over. Church members tend to cluster themselves in groups after the worship is over. They are oblivious to the stranger in their midst while busy talking with their peers. We have lost touch with Jesus' words that said, "I was a stranger and you welcomed me."

To open the door of our hearts we need solitude. Solitude deals with the compulsive self that compels us to seek control, security, and affection. People group themselves together for the purpose of security and affection. To reach out to a stranger means that we need to come out of our comfort zone. We rather deal with the familiar than the unknown. Solitude helps us to gain access to the true self. The true self frees us from the need to impress or please others in our lives. This allows us to serve the community with no hidden agenda or ulterior motive. For the community to grow, communication and communion are essential. Solitude and silence will deepen communication and communion among members of the community.

## Questions for Reflection and Discussion

1. Why did the early Christians take hospitality seriously? Is this tradition practiced today?
2. What are the things that prevent you from creating a space in your hearts for others?
3. How can solitude help you to be a more hospitable person?
4. Who are the strangers in your midst today that the church can extend her welcome?

## Chapter 7

# SOLITUDE AND SILENCE

Go and sit in your cell and your cell will teach you everything.

—ABBA MOSES[1]

Settle yourself in solitude and you will come to Him in yourself.

—TERESA OF AVILA[2]

### The Desert Way of Salvation

ABBA ARSENIUS WAS AN educated man employed by emperor Theodosius to tutor his sons, Arcadius and Honorius. One day he prayed asking the Lord to lead him in the way of salvation. The words came back calling him to flee the world in order to be saved. Arsenius left Rome and sailed to Alexandria. From there he entered the desert and lived a solitary life. Arsenius again prayed, "Lord, lead me in the way of salvation," and again he heard the voice calling on him saying, "Arsenius, flee, be silent, pray always, for these

---

1. Ward, trans. *The Sayings of the Desert Fathers*, 139.
2. Cited by Foster, *Celebration of Discipline*, 96.

are the sources of sinlessness." Solitude, silence, and prayer were the three disciplines that constituted the spirituality of the desert.[3]

The desert fathers, in the fourth and fifth century, saw society as a sinking ship. They swam to a place of safety to avoid spiritual disaster instead of drifting along and allowing society to mold and shape them. The desert happened to be such a place of salvation for their souls. Solitude and silence in the desert freed them from the illusions of the false self. The temptations that Jesus faced in the desert set the example for many to follow in his footsteps. The temptations appealed to his sense of self and identity. Jesus had to battle hard not to allow himself to be fabricated by the compulsions of the world. The three temptations of Jesus in the wilderness had to do with his need for security and survival (turning stone into bread); his need for esteem and affection (jumping from a high tower for a spectacular, heroic show); and his need for power and control (he would be given the kingdoms of the world with their authority and splendor).[4]

Our sense of self and identity are nurtured by our perpetual cravings for security, control, and affection. We work to survive. Work also gives us a sense of security. Money will buy us power and influence. We derive esteem and affection from having friends. It is no wonder that the world views success (and happiness) in terms of work, money, and friends.[5] Work will keep us busy, money will gives us freedom, and having good connections will show our importance. The world will view us poorly if we lack money, do not have influential friends, and not keeping ourselves busy. The false self seeks continual affirmation and admiration from significant others in our life. Our self image is dependent on what others think of us. Our identity is imaged after the world and not after God.

---

3. Nouwen, *The Way of the Heart*, 15.
4. Keating, *The Human Condition*, 13–14.
5. Nouwen, *The Way of the Heart*, 23.

# SOLITUDE AND SILENCE

## Dealing with the False Self

Henri Nouwen, a noted spiritual writer, points out that this false self is dictated by anger and greed:

> When my sense of self depends on what others say of me, anger is a quite natural reaction to a critical word. And when my sense of self depends on what I can acquire, greed flares up when my desires are frustrated. Thus, greed and anger are the brother and sister of a false self fabricated by the social compulsions of an unredeemed world.[6]

The parable of the Prodigal Son tells the story of a father with two sons: one is greedy of his father's wealth and the other is angry at his father's benevolence (Luke 15:11–32).[7] Both carry a false self fabricated by the compulsions of the world. The younger son is greedy of his father's wealth and wants a share of his inheritance. Unwilling to wait any longer, he boldly requests for his share of inheritance. Surprisingly his father agrees to let him have his part. He spends his wealth in wild living and squanders his money away. He loses all he has and is in great need. Before long he finds himself feeding the pigs at a farm. The elder brother is angry that his father slaughters a fattened calf to celebrate the younger son's homecoming. He deserves the celebration more than his prodigal brother who has squandered the father's wealth. It is unfair for him to endure all the hard work, while his younger brother is enjoying life patronizing prostitutes!

## Abandonment of Speech

How can we deal with greed and anger in our life? The beginning step is to learn to empty our life of the false self. According to Thomas Merton, the person who has found solitude is empty, as if he has been emptied by death.[8] We need to empty ourselves of the false self in order for the true self to emerge. When Jesus speaks of

---

6. Ibid., 23.
7. Mah, *Being Truly Human*, 17–18.
8. Merton, *New Seeds of Contemplation*, 81.

his death he reminds his audience about a kernel of wheat falling to the ground. If it doesn't die it will remain a single seed; if it dies it will produce many more seeds. Death leads to new life. One way to empty ourselves is the abandonment of control. The desert has a clever way in doing that. The silence and solitude one encounters in the desert will lead to the abandonment of self.[9] The first thing we learn in the abandonment of self is to die to speech. Language is often used as an agent of control. We use words to manipulate, influence, and propagate. No wonder silence is painful and unbearable to many of us. Stephen Kurtz, looking from a psychoanalyst's point of view, writes:

> In renouncing speech . . . we yield up something fundamentally human—a central means for declaring and expressing our existence. It is a kind of annihilation. Viewed this way, silence is equated to death. To discover that our lives are "rooted in silence that is not death but life" one must first keep quiet.[10]

It is difficult to for us to not to speak when we have to explain or justify our actions. Suppose someone misunderstands my actions. I will take pains to explain why I was acting in that manner to justify that I was not wrong. It is not easy to keep quiet and take the blame. Our reputation is at stake. The more defensive we are in our speech, the more we subject ourselves to the compulsions of the world. Dying to speech is not easy for us because we are fearful of losing control.

It is important to point out the role silence plays in solitude. The classical writers used to speak of solitude and silence as a single entity. They are inseparable. Without silence there will be no solitude. Silence strengthens solitude and completes it. Solitude sets the condition for us to die to speech. The false self in us will slowly wither away when we have no one to talk to. This does not mean that we keep quiet all the time. There are people who take this discipline to the extreme and will stop talking for long periods of time.

---

9. Mah, *Garden of the Soul*, 75–78.
10. Kurtz, "Silence" 137.

## SOLITUDE AND SILENCE

The discipline of solitude and silence will mold us to know when to speak and when not to speak. According to the Psalmist, words fitly spoken are like apples of gold in silver frames. "Much that is unnecessary," wrote Bonhoeffer, "remains unsaid. But the essential and helpful thing can be said in a few words."[11] We will use our speech not to manipulate or propagate but to communicate with grace and understanding when our tongue is under our control, .

### Abandonment of Neighbor

The desert trains us to die to our neighbor.[12] We tend to view ourselves through the lens of others. The compulsive preoccupation with what others think of us means that we are dealing with a self-image that needs constant mending. The desert is indifferent to all this panting for attention. There is no gallery for the false self to play to; there is no audience. All is emptiness. We are free to be ourselves when there is no one to applaud or criticize us. We are not bothered by how or what people think of us because we do not subject ourselves to the dictates of others. We are indeed free when we die to our neighbor. Take the example of Abba Moses:

A magistrate in the city was keen to meet Abba Moses for he heard that he was a devout person. He came to the desert with the aim to search for him. He asked to see the father when he met the first person he came across. The man told the magistrate not to waste his time looking for the old monk for he would be disappointed. He quietly whispered to him that this Abba Moses was a fraud and a heretic. He was not what people said he was. He urged the magistrate not to search further but to return home. This new revelation deeply disappointed him. The magistrate returned home to his friends and relatives. He was keen to bring down the reputation of this monk before them. Then someone asked him to describe exactly the person he met in the desert. "Was he by chance a tall black man?" he asked. The magistrate replied in the

---

11. Bonhoeffer, *Life Together*, 80.
12. Mah, *Garden of the Soul*, 77.

affirmative. He was told that the man he met was indeed Abba Moses. The magistrate went away greatly edified.[13]

Solitude that abandons the false self will help us to gain access to the true self. When we are alone we begin to discover who we are. It is easy for us to forget who we are when we are part of a crowd. Thomas a Kempis quoted someone who once said: "If ever I go among men, I come back less of a man."[14] He also cited the apostle John saying that those who wanted to attend to their inner life must learn to withdraw from the crowd as Jesus did with his disciples. Kierkegaard wrote that solitude was the only way for him to sustain his soul in a culture ruled by the crowd. The solitary does not need to perform or seek approval from others. He has no audience to impress, no authorities to please, and no expectations to meet. He is free to be himself.[15] The man who lives in the midst of the crowd is not free. Merton has this to say about the mass-man:

> Each individual in the mass is insulated by thick layers of insensibility. He doesn't care, he doesn't hear, he doesn't think. He does not act, he is pushed. He does not talk, he produces conventional sounds when stimulated by the appropriate noises. He does not think, he secretes cliches."[16]

## Solitude Leads to Community

The false self that is dictated by greed and anger will lead to the breakdown of community. Solitude that separates us from community will lead us back to serve the community even better. Solitude is not an end to itself. It is not to escape from the world or stay away from people. Conversely, true solitude that is driven by a desire to love God and men will lead us back to community. "We do not go into the desert to escape people," declared Merton, "but to learn how to find them . . . to find out the way to do them the

---

13. Ward, trans., *The Sayings of the Desert Fathers*, 140.
14. Kempis, *The Imitation of Christ*, 65.
15. Lane, *Backpacking with the Saints*, 75–76.
16. Merton, *New Seeds of Contemplation*, 55.

## SOLITUDE AND SILENCE

most good."[17] Communication and communion are essential for a community to thrive well. Unfortunately this is not possible in a society that lacks solitude and silence. A person, subjected to the stimuli of the world through an unending flow of hollow words and noise, is pulled apart and loses its inner center. He finds it hard to distance himself in order to speak to the needs and questions of the world in an effective manner.

### Communication through Silence

Nouwen confessed that the more he spoke the more he needed silence to remain faithful to what he had to say.[18] Silence opens a space in our hearts for the words of God to be received and obeyed. It is out of this obedient space that we are able to communicate and share with others. To speak well does not need the use of many words. Sometimes not speaking is more powerful than speech. Archbishop Theophilus came to the desert to speak to Abba Pambo. But he remained silent and did not say a word to the archbishop. When asked why he did not speak to edify the archbishop, he replied: "If he is not edified by my silence, he will not be edified by my speech."[19]

I remember those times when I was at a loss for words. I had difficulty talking to someone who had just lost a loved one. I was sent there to give consolation, but I struggled using the right words to console a grieving person. I knew that I had to say something. I was searching hard in my mind what to say in a situation like this. The words that came out might sound nice, comforting, and even pastoral, but it did not touch the heart. They sounded hollow, shallow, and superficial. It was mind-talk. Sometimes a better option is to feel and share grief with the other person in silence. It is better not to say anything at all if we cannot find words to say. Shared

---

17. Ibid., 80.
18. Nouwen, *Genesee Diary*, 134.
19. Ward, trans., *The Sayings of the Desert Fathers*, 65.

silence is better than careless speech.[20] Belden Lane shared how the power of silence could connect and heal:

> As our guests arrived later in the week, I was curious to notice how we related to each other in this common observance of silence... We smiled and nodded in passing, but refrained from small talk and niceties ordinarily expected in polite society. As a result, something unusual began to occur. Instead of ignoring these people, I found myself oddly caring for them, valuing their presence without even knowing their names. I started praying for them during the offices, looking forward to their being present even when nothing apparently passed between us. I'd never related to other people in such a way, connected by nothing more than a deliberate silence.[21]

## Communion through Solitude

Solitude gives us the freedom to be ourselves. We do not have to compete and compare with others. We no longer need to seek the approval of others and to cling to them in a unhealthy relationship. Such relationships are based on needs and tend to be exploitative. We use people for our own fulfillment. We do not value the individual person's unique features and see them as different from us. Solitude makes communion possible because it enlarges our capacity to love and serve others. "Love," wrote Rainer Maria Rilke, "consists in this, that two solitudes protect and border and salute each other."[22] True communion is shared friendship between individuals. They are bonded together by a common love for God and people.

Nouwen, in *Reaching Out*, recalls a time when a student came to visit him. He came not to seek any help but simply to spend time with him. They were silent for some minutes after some time of ordinary chatter. Both of them were aware of a presence embracing

---

20. Mah, *Being Truly Human*, 51.
21. Lane, *Solace of Fierce Landscapes*, 223.
22. Rilke, *Letters to a Young Poet*, 59.

## SOLITUDE AND SILENCE

them as the silence grew longer and deeper. Finally the man broke the silence. The following was the conversation between the two of them.

> "It is good to be here" and I said, "Yes, it is good to be together again,"and after that we were silent again for a long period. And as a deep peace filled the empty space between us he said hesitantly, "When I look at you it is as if I am in the presence of Christ." I did not feel startled, surprised or in need of protesting, but I could only say, "It is the Christ in you, who recognizes the Christ in me." "Yes," he said, "He is indeed in our midst,"and then he spoke the words which entered into my soul as the most healing words I had heard in many years, "From now on, wherever you go, or wherever I go, all the ground between us will be holy ground." And when he left I knew that he had revealed to me what community really means.[23]

Nouwen believes that solitude deepens affection and is also the place where real community can take place. Shared solitude strengthens each other through mutual respect, careful consideration to each other's individuality, giving space to each other's privacy, and a deep reverent understanding of the sacredness of the human heart.[24] He further writes:

> In this solitude we encourage each other to enter into the silence of our innermost being and discover there the voice that calls us beyond the limits of human togetherness to a new communion. In this solitude we can slowly become aware of a presence of him who embraces friends and lovers and offers us the freedom to love each other, because he first loved us (1 John 4:19).[25]

---

23. Nouwen, *Reaching Out*, 45–46.
24. Ibid., 44.
25. Ibid., 44.

## The Practice of Solitude and Silence

Most of us do not live in a desert. We can instead detour daily to a solitary place to pray in silence and solitude. One day a monk asked Abba Moses for a word of wisdom. "Go and sit in your cell and your cell will teach you everything," he told him.[26] The monk, when confined to a time of solitude and silence in the cell, would open a space in his heart for God to teach him the way of the desert. Sitting in solitude and silence has a way of wearing down our strong sense of self due to our attachment to things, people, and ideas. Blaise Pascal, French mathematician and Christian philosopher, once wrote that all the unhappiness of men arises from one single fact: that they cannot stay quietly in their own room.[27]

The practice of solitude and silence is a challenge for us who live in an age of hurry.[28] We lack the patience to sit still in the cell for long. An inner world of chaos opens up in us the moment we shut the outer world of noise and people behind us. Shutting the door behind us does not mean that we have gotten rid of the world. We carry the world into our solitude and silence. We give up the practice easily when distracted by all these noises and thoughts in our head. We want to get busy again so that it will shield us from the inner chaos. It is difficult to be alone because the inner thoughts of feelings, fantasies, ideas, memories, and desires are like the wild beasts that keep assaulting us. They keep knocking at our mind's door and will not leave us alone.

How to get rid of them? The trick is not to pay attention to them. We must not fight against these intruding thoughts and feelings. We acknowledge their existence and let them pass by. Suppose a familiar face passes by when I am in deep conversation with another person. I will acknowledge her presence with a nod and continue to talk to my friend. The knocking, after some time, will diminish if I do not open the door and let in the visitors. The

---

26. Ward, trans., *The Sayings of the Desert Fathers*, 139.

27. Pascal, *Pensees*, 42.

28. Material in this section is taken from my book, *Garden of the Soul*, 78–81.

visitors will slowly fade away. The knocking becomes less but it will not go away altogether. We can only reap its benefits if we persevere to stay put in the cell.

## Guidelines to Follow

There is no one correct or best way to observe this discipline. Each person is different in temperament and personality and has to find her own niche. Nevertheless, for those who want to grow in this discipline, certain guidelines need to be observed. First of all, we must be committed to exercising this discipline on a regular basis. We will not reap any benefit out of it if we do it on an ad hoc or inconsistent basis. Rhythm and flow are critical to the progress of any spiritual discipline. We need to do it at least once a day. It is also essential that we practice this discipline in a familiar place and at a fixed time. Changing place and time often will disrupt the rhythm and flow needful for growth in the discipline.

The place must be free from all kinds of distractions. A room or space cluttered with things is not conducive because it reminds us of unfinished tasks that need our attention. If we do not have the luxury to afford an uncluttered space, we can do our solitude and silence early in the morning when the place is still dark. In this way, we will not notice the things around us. The place must be free from all sources of distracting noises coming from the phone, radio, and television. God alone will have our attention in solitude and silence.

The place must be well ventilated with a good flow of fresh air so that we can stay alert. The air temperature is also important because too cold or too warm will bring physical discomfort. The spot chosen to settle down for the discipline must be comfortable but not too comfortable to the body. Sleep and drowsiness may be induced by too comfortable a spot. Any physical discomfort caused by the environment can be a distraction and a hindrance to the practice of solitude and silence. We may need to experiment with various spots in the house to get the optimal space for our discipline. We must try to stick to it as long as we can once we have decided on a spot.

Our posture should keep us alert at all times. We need to experiment with various postures and choose one that is optimal to the discipline. A posture that will keep us alert and not induce us to sleep or feel lazy is the right one. I find that kneeling with my back straight and having a pillow underneath my legs will keep me comfortable and alert at the same time. We should also pay attention to our breathing. Deep, correct breathing will help the body to relax and the mind to be attentive.

How long should we spend in solitude and silence? We should begin in baby steps. A few minutes at the beginning is sufficient. As we progress, we can increase the time to about twenty minutes to half an hour a day. Time passes quickly when we get deeper into the practice of solitude and silence. It is good to end this time by saying the Lord's Prayer aloud. We may want to continue this time with verbalized prayers, praises, and petitions to God.

We should not have expectations during this time of silent prayer. To expect something is to orient our minds or thoughts to something else other than God. Our attention, or rather our intention, should be on God and not on our thoughts, feelings, or concepts. We should reach God with pure faith. It is not easy to let go of our thoughts to reach God with pure faith. Hence we need something to center ourselves. We need a prayer word to help us open to God and to his presence. The meaning of the prayer word is not important. The use of the prayer word is to express our intention or desire for God. A prayer word like "Jesus," "Father," or "Lord have mercy" can be used. We simply come to God by opening ourselves to him. We must not feel agitated or distracted when unwanted thoughts come knocking at our mind's door. We acknowledge their presence and let them go. If these thoughts keep coming in waves we can use the prayer word to redirect our attention to God.

We should not judge or expect something out of this period of solitude and silence. We may feel that we are wasting our time when nothing has happened. We will see the results later. We need to be patient and persevere in this discipline before we can reap the benefits. Gradually we find ourselves more at ease, more confident,

## SOLITUDE AND SILENCE

and less fearful and anxious. Something has changed inside us without our knowledge. Thomas Keating, in his bestselling book *Open Mind, Open Heart*, has this to say:

> In this prayer God is speaking not to your ears, to your emotions, or to your head, but to your spirit, to your inmost being. There is no human apparatus to understand the language or to hear it. A kind of anointing takes place. The fruits of that anointing will appear later in ways that are indirect: in your calmness, in your peace, in your willingness to surrender to God in everything that happens.[29]

Besides a fixed time and place to practice solitude and silence, we can take advantage of the solitary moments that we encounter during the course of the day. My daily drive to work takes about five minutes. It is a scenic drive along a coastal road. During this short drive I will not turn on the car radio or play music. I use this time to remain silent and enjoy a solitary time with God. There are other solitary moments if we care to notice them. A slow walk around the neighborhood just to break away from the routine of work is such a moment. We can use solitary moments like waiting in a clinic to see the doctor or the slowness of a traffic jam to be alone with God.

We need solitude to sustain our soul. Solitude opens a space in our hearts for the true self to emerge. We discover who we are when we are alone. It is difficult to find our true self in a crowd. This was the reason why Jesus habitually withdrew from the crowd whenever he could. Solitude allows the Word of God to be received and obeyed. In solitude Jesus listened to the Father in order to carry out his mission to the world. Solitude is not a means to escape from the world. It is to detach from the world in order to serve the world better. Solitude gives us the freedom to be true to ourselves without the need to compete and compare with others. Only the true self is capable of affection which is needed for us to love self, God, and neighbor.

---

29. Keating, *Open Mind, Open Heart*, 83.

At the same time, the true self lives life at the Center. The modern person, rootless and adrift, carries multiple identities and has many competing selves. He finds it hard to simplify his life when pulled by different obligations from many quarters. He lacks the freedom to say No which sometimes is necessary and needful for him to say Yes to God. We need simplicity to love and obey God. Lacking inner integration, we find ourselves listening to the competing voices that cause our lives to be anxious, hurried, and less peaceful. These will complicate our lives. Listening to the voice within will help us to live life at the Center. Only by yielding to the Center can outward simplicity be achieved.

## Questions for Reflection and Discussion

1. Do you view success in terms of work, money, and influence? What is your definition of success?
2. Do you agree with Kierkegaard that solitude is the only way to sustain his soul in a culture ruled by the crowd?
3. Do you agree that silence and solitude do help in establishing community? Why?
4. What prevent you for having a time of solitude and silence? What are you going to do with these hindrances?

*Chapter 8*

# THE SIMPLE LIFE

There are two wings on which man soars away from earthly things—single-mindedness and purity.

—THOMAS A KEMPIS[1]

## Relinquish Goods and Ego

HIKERS LIKE TO COMPARE notes with fellow hikers while walking the trail. Where have you been? How was the trip? Where would be your next destination? I met a young British girl who had traveled to many places. She had been hiking to countries in Latin America, Europe, and Australia. In Asia she had been to the islands of Phuket and Bali. She told me that she had visited Penang once. I asked her whether she had tasted our "laksa" or "char koay teow". Penangnites are proud of their street food. Subash, my Nepali hiking partner, jokingly asked whether she had tasted the durian, the king of fruits. He said the fruit "smells like hell and tastes like heaven!" Many foreigners I know would rather stay far away from the prickly fruit with a nasty, pungent smell. I told her that she had to try the fruit three times before she could enjoy it.

I noticed that she was a seasoned traveler. She was traveling light for she didn't have a lot of stuff in her backpack. She only

---

1. Kempis, *Imitation of Christ*, 88.

carried the essentials. She loved talking about the many places she had visited on her many hiking trips. I suspect she had a wish list of many more places that she would want to go. Nowadays, it is common for people to have a "bucket list" of things they want to do before they die. After scaling Mount Kinabalu I suddenly had the inspiration to scale the next highest mountain in South East Asia. Climbing mountains or running marathons are like collecting trophies so that we can display them for others to see. It is easy for us to succumb to the consumer mentality that caters to an "incessant thirst for experience, personal achievement, endless distraction, boogie fever."[2] Traveling light, spiritually speaking, is not just to relinquish our goods but our egoistic self as well. We have the tendency to display our unique experiences and achievements to others in order to seek their approval and admiration.

Abba John the Short announced to his brothers that he would be leaving his cell to become an angel. He aspired to become a spiritual giant. He wanted to serve God unceasingly and achieving a higher and deeper ecstatic experience with him. A week later he came back and knocked on the door. "Who's there?" a monk asked. "It's me, John." The monk shouted from behind the door saying, "John's gone off to become an angel; he doesn't live here anymore." He left him outside the door until the next day. When he finally opened the door for John, he said to him, "If you're an angel, keep going; if you're a man, simply get back to your work."[3]

## Freedom to Say No

According to Richard Foster, a theologian and author in the Quaker tradition, we cannot have simplicity without solitude.[4] They go hand in hand. We cannot live the simple lifestyle if we are enslaved to what people think of us. We know, from the previous chapter, that solitude frees us from wanting approval or acclaim from others. Our actions are often prompted by the expectations of significant others

2. Lane, *Backpacking with the Saints*, 86.
3. Ward, *Sayings of the Desert Fathers*, 82.
4. Foster, *Freedom of Simplicity*, 14–15.

## THE SIMPLE LIFE

in our life. We want to keep up with our neighbors and friends. My previous house had a large garden at the back. Mowing the grass was difficult because part of the back garden was on a slope. I would procrastinate the mowing until the last minute. I noticed that there were times when I was prompted to cut the grass because my neighbor cut his. Other times, he took the cue from me when I cut mine. It is difficult to live the simple lifestyle if we are competing with each other. In order to look good before others we need to adopt a lifestyle that is comparable to our friends and neighbors. Our neighbor's new car may prompt us to think of having a new one. Our car suddenly looks "old" and needs changing. Conversely, we may do the exact opposite. In order for people to admire our simplicity, we go out of the way to own things that are bought from a thrift store or a garage sale. We want to show off our simplicity to the world. Yet, our self-consciousness betrays our desire to live simply.

It is this self-consciousness that also prevents us from saying No to the requests made by others. Most of the time when people asked me to preach I would say Yes. Sometimes I regretted saying Yes because I found out later that it conflicted with a more important schedule. There were times when a better offer was made and I had to reject it because of prior commitment. It takes courage for us to say No. Even when we say No we are obliged to give reasons or excuses for rejecting the offer. I am sure most of us have this experience. We need to know that sometimes our No can mean Yes. When we say No to a request we are free to say Yes to the things we really want to do for God. Eugene Peterson gives us this advice:

> No is a freedom word. I don't have to do what either my glands or my culture tell me to do. The judicious, well-placed No frees me from many a blind alley, many a rough detour, frees us from debilitating distractions and seductive sacrilege. The art of saying No sets us free to follow Jesus.[5]

---

5. Peterson, *Subversive Spirituality*, 12.

## Freedom to Let Go

One of the conditions to follow Jesus is to live a life of simplicity. The Bible warns us many times about the accumulation of wealth and possessions. They can be a snare to our souls. Simplicity is more than just having possessions. The poor may not have much but some poor people are not simple in terms of handling wealth or possessions. It is not so much about what we own but about what owns us. We know the proverbial story of a monkey whose hand is caught inside a coconut shell. He struggles to release his hand from inside the shell. He will not be able to free his hand unless he is willing to let go of the precious nut he has in his hand. The opening of the coconut shell is just big enough for his hand to go through without holding the nut. As long as he holds on to the nut he will not be free. Some of us may not have much but we find it difficult to let go because we are attached to our possessions.

The desert monks were known for their solitude and simplicity of life. Life was simple in the desert. They either stayed in a cave or a stone hut with a roof of branches over it. They had a mat for a bed, sheepskin to keep warm, a jar of water to quench thirst, and a lamp to give light. They had a meal a day. The diet included dry bread, water, salt, some oil, and vegetables. Sleep was restricted to a bare minimum. They weaved baskets and mats for a living. They followed a rhythm of work and prayer. The simple, uncluttered life served them well in seeking after God.

After Abba Euprepius found out that his cell was emptied by robbers he ran after them. He followed them not to get back his belongings but to give them his walking stick. Apparently the robber had missed the stick standing at the corner of his cell. When asked the reason for his abnormal behavior, he replied, "We must accept it with joy and gratitude, realizing that we have been set free from care." This desert monk had learned well the lesson of letting go.

*THE SIMPLE LIFE*

## Rooted at the Center

It is difficult for us to live the life of simplicity. We will fail if we decide to live the simple life based on changing the external circumstances. The external circumstances are like the raging sea. Our life, like a boat, will drift along by the outer distractions of life if it is not properly anchored to the seabed below. We remain rootless. Rootedness, according to Simone Weil, is the most important and least recognized need of the human soul.[6] We will try to be several selves at once if we lack inner integration. The modern person, lacking integration, lives in many worlds and plays different roles at any one time. He picks up different identities along the way.

## Many Competing Selves

If we ask a modern person who he is, he will answer in many different ways depending on who he is talking to. He can identify himself vocationally by saying he is a teacher or doctor. In terms of his use of leisure time he may say that he is a golfer or tennis player. He may proclaim that he is married, divorced or a single parent if he wants to identify himself in terms of his social status. He can identify himself as an environmentalist or anti-abortionist. Religiously, he may declare that he is a Buddhist, Christian or Atheist. It is indeed hard to live the simple life in the light of so many competing selves. Richard Foster in *Freedom of Simplicity* shares this dilemma:

> You may be wondering what all this has to do with simplicity. Perhaps I could explain it this way. Within all of us is a whole conglomerate of selves . . . Each one screams to protect his or her vested interests. If a decision is made to spend a relaxed evening listening to Chopin, the business self and the civic self rise up to protest at the loss of precious time. The energetic self paces back and forth, impatient and frustrated, and the

---

6. Weil, *The Need for Roots*, 3.

religious self reminds us of the lost opportunities for study or evangelistic contact.⁷

Outward simplicity can only be achieved if we live life from the Center. If our life is integrated at the Center then the competing selves we have will be orientated to the Center and under its unifying control. So our focus is not in achieving a simple life outwardly but concentrating on living life at the Center. We no longer feel the pull of many obligations and our Yes or No is not based on reason or excuse but from the "basis of inner guidance and whispered promptings from the Center of our life."⁸ We will find our life unhurried, calm, and with confidence.

## To Will One Thing

We must first have inward simplicity in order to have outward simplicity. To achieve inward simplicity we need to will one thing. According to Kierkegaard, the 19th century Danish theologian and philosopher, we cannot have purity of heart or inward simplicity if our mind is divided. This understanding is based on a verse from Scripture that says: "Come near to God and he will come near to you. Wash your hands, you sinners and purify your hearts, you double minded" (James 4:8). When we make work to be the most important thing in our lives, we will find that there are other competing needs that conflict with work. The needs of the family and other social obligations will take time away from our work. In this case our mind is divided between our obligations to work and to the family. Those who are workaholics can understand what I mean. The only way to achieve purity of heart or an undivided mind is to will one thing - the Good. Any other focus will lead us to a divided mind and an unfulfilled life. The Good, to Kierkegaard, is God himself who is the unifying principle in all his creation. Anything outside of God is not to will the one thing but a multiple of things that lead to a divided and corrupt mind. If we do good out of fear that we will not be in God's good book, or if we

---

7. Foster, *Freedom of Simplicity*, 95–96.
8. Kelly, *A Testament of Devotion*, 100.

do good out of getting a reward or favor from others, then we have not will the one thing.

How can we live life at the Center? We must satisfy one condition first. We must *really want to* put this as the main focus of our life - to will the one thing. We must continually listen to the Voice or Holy that resides in the holy sanctuary of our soul. Thomas Kelly, a well known spiritual speaker and writer, in *A Testament of Devotion* writes on what it takes to live life at the Center:

> Deep within us all there is an amazing inner sanctuary of the soul, a holy place, a Divine Center, a speaking Voice, to which we may continually return ... Yielding to these persuasions, gladly committing ourselves in body and soul, utterly and completely, to the Light Within, is the beginning of the true life.[9]

## Listen to the Inner Voice

We need to take heed to the words of Jesus that call on us to seek first his kingdom and his righteousness and all other things will be given to us as well (Matt 6:33). We are often anxious over the things that are essential for our living. We usually pay close attention to these things first. The proper order is to pay close attention to do God's will first through listening to him who dwells within us. Listening to the Voice or Light within will mute all the competing voices that are trying to get our attention. This simplifies our life and causes us to be less anxious, more peaceful, and unhurried. Life from the Center is "vastly richer and deeper than all this hurried existence, a life of unhurried serenity and peace and power ... where the fretful calls of life are integrated, where No as well as Yes can be said with confidence."[10]

Kelly gives an example of John Woolman who ordered his outward life by listening to the inner voice. Woolman was a businessman. He felt a need to do something about his business when he found that his business was growing every year. It had nothing

9. Ibid., 3.
10. Ibid., 115–16.

to do with a more affluent life due to the increased earnings. He knew in his heart that he was not tempted with more wealth. He had been contented with living a simple life all the while. He had problems with two issues that bothered him. The first issue had to do with selling items that catered to the vanity rather than the real needs of the consumers. Woolman wrote in his journal: "Things that served chiefly to please the vain mind in people, I was not easy to trade in; seldom did it; and whenever I did I found it weakened me as a Christian."[11] The other issue was to free himself from the busyness of his business so that he would have more time to serve the Lord. After cutting back his business he was able to engage more fully in a traveling ministry. His ministry had such a great impact on the Quakers that they stopped engaging slaves long before America gained independence from the British Empire.[12] Kelly had this to say about John Woolman:

> His outward life became simplified on the basis of an inner integration . . . He didn't have to struggle, and renounce, and strain to achieve simplicity. He yielded to the Center and his life became simple. It was synoptic. It has singleness of eye. "If thine eye be single thy whole body shall be full of light." His many selves were integrated into a single true self, whose whole aim was humbly walking in the presence and guidance and will of God.[13]

## Steps to Simplify our Lives

True simplicity requires both an outward expression and an inward reality. Our outward display of simplicity is idolatrous and legalistic without the inward reality. It is not possible to have an inward simplicity without our lifestyle impacted by it. When our life is gradually integrated, simplicity takes over and we are able to become less anxious over the goods of life. We are able to hold to these things lightly. Though we own them, they do not own us. We can take concrete

11. Woolman, *The Journal of John Woolman*, 41.
12. Story adapted from Foster, *Freedom of Simplicity*, 86–87.
13. Kelly, *A Testament of Devotion*, 94.

# THE SIMPLE LIFE

steps to simplify our lives while paying attention to life at the Center. What are the steps we can take to simplify our lives further?[14] I can think of five areas where we can simplify our lives. The five areas are: possessions, space, speech, technology, and time.

## Our Possessions

The first area we need to simplify our lives is the things we possess. Our consumerist mentality, if left unchecked, will addict us to accumulate more things that we really need. Some people in my condominium have to rent storage space from the building management to store their goods. Most of the things they store away may not be used at all. They are collecting dust over the years and eventually have to be discarded away. A good rule of thumb is to give or sell away those things we think we will not use for the next three to five years.

When I was in Vancouver I loved going to garage sales. I came home empty-handed most of the time. The purpose of the trip was more like a social outing than bargain hunting. It was interesting to know the things that people possessed around the house. We could make a wild guess about the people who lived in these houses from the things they possessed. Most of the things on displayed were old. I suspected that they were in storage for a long time. A thing that was deemed useless to someone might be of use to another person. To our delight, once a while, we might come across a "gem" that we really needed at that time. Others had the habit of going to garage sales in order to accumulate more things since the things were sold cheaply at such sales. After a while, they too had their own garage sales to get rid of those things they never used.

We need to be aware of impulse buying. Just because an item is on sale and is selling cheap due to stock clearance does not mean that we must have it. We need to ask ourselves whether we need to use this item straightaway. We buy, on impulse, thinking that we can use the item in the near future. The item is usually stored away

---

14. Foster offers ten principles of the expression of simplicity. See *Celebration of Discipline*, 90–95.

and conveniently forgotten. Impulse buying, lured by sophisticated adverts, can be addictive. One way to overcome this addiction is to set a limit on how much we can spend using our cash or credit card. We must try to clear the debt at the end of each month. To live the simple life we need to detach ourselves from the habit of acquiring more possessions than we really need.

## Our Space

The second area we need to simplify our lives is space. Getting rid of some of our unwanted, earthly possessions will help us to get rid of the clutter in our physical space. A cluttered room or office is a reflection of unfinished tasks or a lack of discipline in organization. A simple life needs to begin with the physical space first. In chapter 6, I mention that the physical space can have a psychological and emotional impact on our lives. A room free of clutter provides lots of empty spaces that can have a calm and soothing effect on its occupants. We may have noticed that the empty spaces between trees give the forest its serene nature. A simple life that is unhurried and peaceful will thrive well in an organized space free from unnecessary clutter.

We need space to be alone. We know that busyness complicates our life. Our minds are cluttered with the many things that need our attention at once. We are pulled in different directions by the competing demands made on us. It is good to take time off even for a short period of time in the midst of a busy schedule. We need a psychological space to be alone for sanity's sake. We have to take our minds away from the stream of consciousness that are congested with ongoing tasks and deadlines. A slow walk away from office or home may help us to get rid of the things that are cluttering our minds. Walking alone will free our minds from the exchanges of work, goods, and information that feed our ego. A simple life needs psychological and emotional space to thrive well.

# THE SIMPLE LIFE

## Our Speech

The third area we need to simplify our lives is speech. The wrong use of words can complicate our life. Try not to use negative words for these will invoke negative feelings in us and also to those who hear us speak. Paul exhorts us to let our conversation be full of grace and seasoned with salt (Col 4:6). A kind word will go a long way to lift the spirit of the downcast. James reminds us of the dangers of uncontrolled speech. Words wrongly spoken can be a spark that cause a forest fire. Someone says that when we speak out of anger we will make the best speech we will ever regret. What we eat is passed out but we cannot take back the words we have spoken. If is better for us to control our tongue and speak less. Speak honestly and mean what we say. Try to avoid gossip and slander as far as possible. We need to pay close attention to our speech if we want to live the simple life.

We must also learn to say No. Life becomes complicated when we say Yes to the requests others make on us. We find less time for ourselves when our schedule is crowded out by the many requests that demand our attention. It is difficult for us to say No because of the guilt feelings that we have let down the person who makes the request. There are some guidelines we can take in answering to the requests of others.[15] We should avoid desperate requests. We should not yield to the urgent request if we are asked to decide right away and not given enough time to think over. We may want to suggest another person to take up the request if we know of someone who is available and capable of doing the job. In this way we are giving the the other person the opportunity to serve and grow as well. We should pick the one we think we can do a better job if we have to choose between two tasks. We should not pick the one that gives us more status or recognition. We can set limit and ration our time. We have the right to refuse the request if the request does not fit with our allotted time. It is important that when we refuse a request we should not feel guilty about it.

---

15. Hummel, *Freedom from Tyranny of the Urgent*, 63.

# Take Up Your Mat and Walk

## Our Use of Technology

The fourth area we need to simplify our lives is technology. Technology can be subversive if we are not careful. The mechanical clock was invented by a monk. The clock helped the monks to tell time so that they could devote themselves consistently and regularly to the worship of God during the course of the day. This technology is now used more for the accumulation of wealth than for religious duties.[16] Digitized technology helps us to get connected instantly. The smart phone is a useful tool for us to connect with people far and near. I can speak to my son, who lives in Canada, by audio or video through the use of apps installed in my smart phone. We are blessed with such convenient and time-saving devices. We can stay connected all the time because of this free and easy access,.

It is a common sight nowadays to see families eating at the same table in a restaurant with everybody's eyes glued to the small screen. Meal times are the best occasions for conversations to take place. Yet, this is not happening to many families. Dad may be checking his updates on the latest gossip in Facebook, mum may want to text a friend using Twitter, son is playing games on his phone, and daughter is watching a movie. All the people at the table are busy connected to the internet and yet not connected to each other. It is high time for us not to let technology controls and complicates our life. We must make it a point to stay disconnected for part of the day. We need to ration our time spent on social media. Our hunger for information should be restricted by not turning to the media anytime we want. I know it takes discipline to limit the use of digitized technology in our daily lives. It is so prevalent in our culture that we cannot live without it. Like our possessions, we can own technology but we must not let technology owns us. The simple life requires us to use technology discreetly without being addicted by it.

---

16. Postman, *Technopoly*, 15.

# THE SIMPLE LIFE

## Our Time

The fifth area we need to simplify our lives is time. The Temple of Time in Rome housed the first mechanical clock on display for the first time. Crowds of people waited for hours to take a glimpse of this wonderful invention. They were amazed at this wonderful technology with the elaborate clockworks. Looking at this machine, the people were torn between admiration for the precise machine and suspicion, for they knew that *their* time was no longer theirs.[17] A survey had shown that Canadians worried about time more than money, health, and family.[18] We always complain that we do not have enough time. We feel squeezed by the lack of time. When squeezed for more time, we tend to multitask thinking that we can do two or more things using the same amount of time. In this way we are saving time for something else. Multitasking may not be productive or effective. We usually cannot do a job well when multitasking. In some instances, it can be dangerous. Drivers who drive and talk on the phones are four times more likely to suffer serious crashes.[19] Albert Einstein jokingly made this comment about multitasking: "Any man who can drive safely while kissing a pretty girl is simply not giving the kiss the attention it deserves."

Multitasking may not necessary save precious time. To simplify our lives, we must learn to attend to one task at a time. We can stay focus, in this way, and not be distracted. If we have several tasks that we need to do we can have a priority list. Work with the most important item first and complete it before we go to the next on the list. There is a temptation for us to go to the next item even while we are working on the immediate item on the list. Thich Nhat Hanh has this to say to those who want to live the simple life:

> If while washing dishes, we think only of the cup of tea that awaits us, thus hurrying to get the dishes out of the way as if they were a nuisance... While drinking the cup of tea, we will only be thinking of other things, barely

17. Cousineau, *The Art of Pilgrimage*, 56–57.
18. Righton, " How We Live" 39.
19. Stross, " Caution: Drivers May be Surfing the Web" 3.

aware of the cup in our hands. Thus we are sucked away into the future—and we are incapable of actually living one minute of life.[20]

## Questions for Reflection and Discussion

1. Why is it difficult for you to say No to requests made on you by other people?
2. Why is a simply lifestyle important to you personally?
3. Why is it important for you to live life at the Center? How can you live life at the Center?
4. What are the areas in your life and the steps you think you can take to simplify your life today?

---

20. Hanh, *The Miracle of Mindfulness*, 4-5.

# BIBLIOGRAPHY

Barton, Ruth Harley. *Sacred Rhythms: Arranging Our Lives for Spiritual Transformation*. Downers Grove, IL: IVP, 2006.

Benner, David G. *Presence and Encounter: The Sacramental Possibilities of Everyday Life*. Grand Rapids: Brazos, 2014.

———. *Soulful Spirituality: Becoming Fully Alive and Deeply Human*. Grand Rapids: Brazos, 2011.

———. *Spirituality and the Awakening Self: The Sacred Journey of Transformation*. Grand Rapids: Brazos, 2012.

Berry, Wendell. "Christianity and the Survival of Creation." *Cross Currents* 43/2 (1993).

Bloom, Anthony. *Beginning to Pray*. Mahwah, NJ: Paulist, 1970.

Bonhoeffer, Dietrich. *Life Together*. New York: Harper & Row, 1952.

Canham, Elizabeth J. "A School for the Lord's Service." *Weavings* IX/1 (1994), 11–20.

Cannato, Judy. "Paradox Road." *Weavings* XVI/6 (2001) 39–45.

Chase, Steven. *The Tree of Life: Models of Christian Prayer*. Grand Rapids: Baker, 2005.

Chittister, Joan. *Wisdom Distilled from the Daily: Living the Rule of St. Benedict Today*. New York: HarperSanFrancisco, 1990.

Chrysostom, John. "Homily 45 on Acts" in *A Select Library of the Nicene and Post-Nicene Fathers of the Christian Church*, First Series (vol.11). Edited by Philip Schaff. New York: Christian Literature Company, 1886–90.

Cousineau, Phil. *The Art of Pilgrimage*. Berkeley, CA: Conari, 1998.

Cox, Darrel. "The Physical Body in Spiritual Formation: What God Has Joined Together Let No One Put Asunder." *Journal of Psychology and Christianity*. 21/3 (2002) 281–291.

De Caussade, Jean-Pierre. *The Sacrament of the Present Moment*. New York: HarperSanFrancisco, 1982.

De Waal, Esther. *Lost in Wonder: Rediscovering the Spiritual Art of Attentiveness*. Collegeville, MN: Liturgical, 2003.

———. "Attentiveness." *Weavings* XVII/4 (2002) 20–27.

# BIBLIOGRAPHY

Demarest, Bruce. "Reflections of Developmental Spirituality: Journey Paradigms and Stages." *Journal of Spiritual Formation & Soul* Care 1/2 (2008) 149–167.

DePree, Max. *Leadership is an Art*. New York: Dell, 1989.

Dresner, Samuel H. ed. *I Asked for Wonder: A Spiritual Anthology: Abraham Joshua Heschel*. New York: Crossroad, 1992.

Douglas, Deborah Smith. "C. S. Lewis and our Longing for Home." *Weavings* XV/4 (2000) 6–17.

Edwards, Tilden. *Living in the Presence: Spiritual Exercises to Open Our Lives to the Awareness of God*. New York: HarperSanFrancisco, 1995.

———. *Living Simply through the Day: Spiritual Survival in a Complex Age*. Mahwah, NJ: Paulist, 1998.

Einstein, Albert. *Ideas and Opinions*. Translated by Sonja Bargmanm. New York: Bonanza, 1988.

Foster, Richard J. *Celebration of Discipline: The Path to Spiritual Growth*. New York: HarperSanFrancisco, 1998.

———. *Freedom of Simplicity: Finding Harmony in a Complex World*. New York: HarperSanFrancisco, 2005.

Fraser, Elouise Renich. *Cofessions of a Beginning Theologian*. Downers Grove, IL: IVP, 1998.

Gonzales, Laurence. *Deep Survival*. New York: W. W. Norton, 2003.

Griebner, David M. "The Carpentar and the Unbuilder." *Weavings* II/4 (1987) 24–27.

Gros, Frederic. *A Philosophy of Walking*. London: Verso, 2015.

Hanh, Thich Nhat. *The Miracle of Mindfulness*. London: Rider, 1991.

Heschel, Abraham J. *Man Is Not Alone: A Philosophy of Religion*. New York: Farrer, Straus and Young, 1951.

Hummel, Charles E. *Freedom from Tyranny of the Urgent*. Downers Grove: IVP, 1997.

Jones, Alan. *Soul Making: The Desert Way of Spirituality*. USA: HarperSanFrancisco, 1985.

Keating, Thomas. *Open Mind, Open Heart: The Contemplation of the Gospel*. New York: Continuum, 2004.

———. *The Human Condition: Contemplation and Transformation*. New York: Paulist, 1999.

Kelly, Thomas R. *A Testament of Devotion*. San Francisco: HarperSanFrancisco, 1996.

Kempis, a Thomas. *The Imitation of Christ*. Trans. Betty I. Knott. Glasgow: Collins, 1978.

Kidd, Sue Monk. *God's Joyful Surprise: Finding Yourself Loved*. San Francisco: Harper & Row, 1987.

———. "Live Welcoming to All" *Weavings* 12/5 (1997) 9.

Kurtz, Stephen A. "Silence" *Commonweal*, March 1984, 137.

Lane, Belden C. *Backpacking with the Saints: Wilderness Hiking as Spiritual Practice*. New York: Oxford University Press, 2015.

# BIBLIOGRAPHY

Mah, Mark. *Being Truly Human: The Desert Way of Spiritual Formation*. Eugene, OR: Resource, 2012.

———. *Garden of the Soul: Exploring Metaphorical Landscapes of Spirituality*. Eugene, OR: Wipf & Stock, 2014.

McMartin, Jason. "Sleep, Sloth, and Sanctification" *Journal of Spiritual Formation & Soul Care*. 6/2 (2013) 255–272.

Merton, Thomas. *New Seeds of Contemplation*. New York: New Directions, 1962.

Muir, John. *My First Summer in the Sierra*. New York: Penguin, 1987.

Mulholland, M. Robert. *Invitation to a Journey: A Road Map for Spiritual Formation*. Downers Grove, IL: IVP, 1993.

Norris, Kathleen. *Dakota: A Spiritual Geography*. New York: Ticknor & Fields, 1993.

Nouwen, Henri J. M. *Reaching Out: The Three Movements of the Spiritual Life*. New York: Image, 1975.

———. *The Genesee Diary: Report from a Trappist Monastery*. New York: Doubleday, 1976.

———. *The Way of the Heart: Desert Spirituality and Contemporary Ministry*. New York: Seabury, 1981.

Owens, L. Roger. "Keeping in Touch." *Weavings* XXX/2 (2015) 17–21.

Owens, Tara M. *Embracing the Body: Finding God in Our Flesh and Bone*. Downers Grove, IL: IVP, 2015.

Paintner, Christine Valters. "Cultivating the Eyes of the Heart." *Weavings* XXIX/3 (2014) 27–31.

Palmer, Parker. *A Hidden Wholeness: The Journey Toward an Undivided Life*. San Francisco: Jossey-Bass, 2004.

———. *To Know As We Are Known: Education as Spiritual Journey*. New York: HarperSanFrancisco, 1993.

Pascal, Blaise. *Pensees*. Trans. John Warrington. London: J.M. Dent, 1973.

Peterson, Eugene H. *A Long Obedience in the Same Direction: Spiritual Disciplines for Ordinary People*. Downers Grove, IL: IVP, 1980.

———. *Christ Plays in Ten Thousand Places: A Conversation in Spiritual Theology*. Grand Rapids: Eerdmans, 2005.

———. *Subversive Spirituality*. Grand Rapids: Eerdmans, 1997.

Phillips, Susan S. *The Cultivated Life: From Ceaseless Striving to Receiving Joy*. Downers Grove, IL: IVP, 2015.

Pirrone, Michael C. "What Hiking Does To The Brain Is Pretty Amazing" Wimp.com, April 11, 2016. Online:http://www.wimp.com/what-hiking-does-to-the-brain-is-pretty-amazing/

Pohl, Christine D. *Making Room: Recovering Hospitality as a Christian Tradition*. Grand Rapids: Eerdmans, 1999.

Pollard, C. Williams. *The Soul of the Firm*. Grand Rapids: Zondervan, 1996.

Porter, Steve L. "The Willardian Corpus" *Journal of Spiritual Formation & Soul Care* 3/2 (2010) 239–266.

Postman, Neil. *Technopoly: The Surrender of Culture to Technology*. New York: Knopf, 1992.

# BIBLIOGRAPHY

Rensberger, David. "The Heaven Below: A Spirituality of Small Things" *Weavings* XXIX/3 (2014) 43–47.

———. "The Holiness of Winter" *Weavings* XI/6 (1996) 34–42.

Reps, Paul. *Zen Flesh, Zen Bones*. Garden City: Doubleday, 1961.

Righton, Barbara. "How We Live" *McClean's*. July 1 (2006).

Rilkes, Rainer Maria. *Letters to a Young Poet*. Trans. M.D. Herter. New York: Norton, 1993.

Scazzero, Peter. *Emotionally Healthy Spirituality: Unleash a Revolution in Your Life in Christ*. Nashville: T. Nelson, 2006.

Seitz, Ron. *Song for Nobody, A Memory Vision of Thomas Merton*. Ligouri, MI: Triumph, 1993.

Silf, Margaret. *Companions of Christ: Ignatian Spirituality for Everyday Living*. Grand Rapids: Eerdmans, 2004.

Stross, Randall. "Caution: Driver May Be Surfing the Web" *New York Times*. August 24 (2008) Business.

Thompson, Majorie. *Soul Feast: An Invitation to the Spiritual Life*. Louisville: Westminster John Knox, 1995.

Tonybee, Philip. *Part of a Journey: An Autobiographical Journal - 1977-79*. London: Collins, 1981.

Vanier, Jean. *Becoming Human*. Toronto: Anansi, 1998.

———. *Community and Growth*. New York: Paulist, 1989.

Ward, Benedicta, trans. *The Sayings of the Desert Fathers: The Alphabetical Collection*. Cistercian Studies Series 59. Kalamazoo, MI: Cistercian, 1975.

Weil, Simone. *The Need for Roots: Prelude to a Declaration of Duties Toward Mankind*. Trans. Arthur Willis. New York: Harper Colophon, 1971.

Willard, Dallas. *The Spirit of the Disciplines: Understanding How God Changes Lives*. New York: HarperSanFrancisco, 1991.

Woolman, John. *The Journal of John Woolman*. Secaucus: Citadel, 1971.

www.ingramcontent.com/pod-product-compliance
Lightning Source LLC
Chambersburg PA
CBHW070920160426
43193CB00011B/1541